Stringing Words

Stringing Words

by The Windmill Writers

Edited by
Jane Andrews
Lynn DiGiacomo
Joan Mazzu
Mary O'Brien

With an Introduction by Carla Riccio

The Writing Life Press
Southampton, L.I., N.Y.

The Writing Life Press
Southampton, L.I., N.Y.

Photography and Design by Mary O'Brien
Printed in the United States of America
First Printing November 2009

ISBN 978-1-61658-353-8

Stringing Words

"How do you like to go up in a swing, up in the air so blue? Oh, I do think it the pleasantest thing"... to see fields and forests and foreign lands and "Lands of Counterpane" even while sick in bed. Robert Louis Stevenson taught me to dream big and far, opened doors I didn't even know were there—all in a little book of poems that I still have, cover ripped off, but still having magic—the magic of sending a bottle off in the ocean and imagining another little boy or girl finding it, the magic and power of stringing words together in such a way to move a little girl on a lifelong journey to capture those words and put them on paper.

Lynn DiGiacomo

Acknowledgments

Many thanks to our advisor and coach Carla Riccio. Her suggestions were clear and helpful, and our rewrites were much better for her guidance. Sometimes, by Carla saying little about what we had written, we knew that we could write it better. Over the past years in the group we have benefited from Carla's judgment and suggestions and have learned as well to value the critiques and encouragement of our fellow writers.

The editors wish to extend particular thanks to the authors who have generously allowed us to include their essays in this collection.

We would also like to thank The Rogers Memorial Library in Southampton, N.Y., for extending to our group its hospitality in hosting our workshops. Of course, the opinions and views expressed in this collection are those of the individual writers

Dedication

To Carla Riccio who prompts us to find our voices.

❦ Table of Contents ❧

❧Introduction

In his introduction to *The Best American Essays of 2008*, Adam Gopnick writes that the essayist's task is not to answer the question "How shall we live?" but rather to answer, "What does it feel like to be alive?"

The essays in this volume meet this challenge head on. In these pages, the full texture of life unfolds, detail by detail, and the reader steps into another skin: we become, for a moment, the awed mother watching her grown son's mastery in the kitchen; the nervous first-time dancer swept up by a whirlwind of strangers at a New England barn dance; the late-night tele-shopper mesmerized beyond better judgment; the ten-year-old girl in her hand-sewn apron, anxiously awaiting her turn at the 4-H fashion show.

But this volume marks a greater challenge than the sum of its words. More than any finished piece can show, this work represents an evolution in the lives of its authors. In January 2006, the first Personal Essay Workshop drew together a random collection of hopeful scribblers and closet journalers in a small conference room at the Rogers Memorial Library in Southampton. Over the next three years, the group grew, rough drafts spawned polished gems (and more rough drafts) and the questions asked around the table became more complex. We moved from "What is a memoir?" to "What is the difference between truth and memory?" from "How do I double-space my document?" to "How do I capture a single moment in time?" We had, in short, become a community of real writers.

Bound volumes always have the scent of accomplishment, and this one deserves that distinction. But it's important to note that this book is more milestone than endpoint. The writers gathered here will continue the hard, quiet work of writing—of thrashing through the blank page into that private jungle of memory, fact, and feeling, to discover, again and again, the wild treasures inside.

Carla Riccio
September 2009

❧ Michele Voso ❧

Tre Piccolo Pezzi
(Three Little Pieces)

❧Primo Piccolo Pezzi

"I don't know. I'm not sure just what she was saying, she talks so fast, I can hardly pick out the individual words. I also think she's using a local dialect. But I think she was just complaining about her aches and pains. Something about having to go to the bathroom. You know how old people are, they're always running to the John to pee. And I think she can't eat meat, she said something about *carne*, that's meat? Right? So, I just nodded with a concerned look and said, '*si, si.*' Eventually I will have enough Italian to have a real conversation. I think it's vocabulary. That's the key. I'm going to memorize ten words a day starting right now. Anyway, here's the lettuce she gave me from the garden. It made a beautiful salad and there was almost no dirt on it when I washed it."

"Promises, promises, you have been promising to memorize ten words a day since we started living here. Oh, this salad is beautiful. Um. And tastes good, can't get veggies like this in the States. Okay, so what did she sound like she was saying?"

"I think it sounded like *cano pee pee a lugga. Lavarsi* or something like that. I'm going to get the dictionary and look it up."

"Eat first, it's a great salad. Are those zucchinis from her garden too?"

"Yup. I'm going to use them for dinner tonight. Sliced thin, fried in olive oil with garlic served over penne or farfalle.

A little dusting of Parmagiano? Right? All right, back to what she said — here's the dictionary, we can read it while we eat."

"Okay, okay. But don't let the salad get wilted."

"Yes, okay but...to the job at hand, now we know what pee pee is and I think — let me see if I remember — yes, it sounded like either *carne* or *cane*. Okay, it's either meat or dog. Does that sound right? Oh, I know, Alfie was there, maybe she wasn't the one that's sick, maybe it's Alfie. That's it. *Cane.* 'Dog.' *Cane* pee pee. Now I'll look up *lugga*. I hope it's not what Lucca had, that urinary tract infection. Do boy dogs get that kind of thing?"

"I don't know, I think you are off on a tangent. Why don't you just eat first and do that later. Don't waste this salad."

"All right, all right. Oh, wait, it's not, oh, I see, it's wash, *lavabo,* 'clean.' "

"What's that, what are you doing? Stop that. Don't spit that lettuce all over the place. Stop."

"*Cane* pee pee, wash the lettuce. It wasn't *lugga* it was *latuga.* Lettuce. That's what she said: 'The dog pee peed on the lettuce. Wash it.' "

❧ Secondo Piccolo Pezzi

"It's lucky you didn't run after you grabbed his wallet. We would have had a hard time explaining that behavior."

"But really, that's a little odd. You have to admit—Financial Police– chasing you to see if you kept your receipt. Italy is a beautiful, wonderful, magical country, but, I just can't get used to their little, quirky laws. Imagine telling people they have to keep receipts for every purchase, from a scoop of gelato to an Armani suit, within a hundred feet of the shop and be ready to show it on demand to the Financial Police. I forgot all about that little law—so how did I know that's what they wanted from you. They looked like young hoods, to me."

"So you automatically assumed that he had taken my wallet!"

"Well, it looked just like your wallet. Black leather, had his photo ID where you keep your license, how did I know he was just showing me his police ID? And you had that funny look on your face, like something had just happened. I just put two and two together."

"Something did just happen, my wife tried to steal the wallet of a cop and was just about to be arrested. And you did just put two and two together and you came up with five. You were always bad with numbers. We're lucky they had a sense of humor. I would have gotten a big fine for not taking my receipt for a slice of pizza; but you deserved to do hard time for snatching a wallet from a tax cop."

"Well, that law is a bit extreme, don't you think? Chasing people through the streets… and..."

"Darling, we've been living in Italy, on and off for over eleven years. If we've only learned one thing, it's that as countries go, Italy is one of your more...quirky countries. Wouldn't you agree? "

"Yes, cara mia, d'acordo."

∽ Terzo Piccolo Pezzi

Shopping in Italy is always fun. Even if it's just for a few groceries in a local *bottega*. The food that everyone in Italy takes for granted—thinly cut proscuitto, delicious breads, *Parmesan* and *Romano* cheeses—are available everywhere, are fairly priced, and are always of the highest quality. My husband and I have always prided ourselves on our skill at purchasing food. We are well-versed in the local specialties in the area where we have our little house. We know our metric weights and measures (sort of), and the local shopkeepers seem to enjoy our company when we shop, as do our neighbors when we meet them occasionally while waiting our turn to be served.

To be truthful, my Italian is not what it should be, but I never let that stop me. I'm particularly proud of my ability to handle myself in a food store, and last week I waited patiently for my turn on a particularly crowded morning and my turn finally came up. Feeling confident, I proceeded to place my order: "*una etto prosuitto, metza kilo parmagiano reggiano, quatro pannini*, and yogurt, peach please." "*Come?*" "Peach," said I in Italian in my little mouse voice, since I felt panic taking over. I don't think you can imagine what it is like when ten or twelve *donna veccio* (old ladies) start laughing and repeating what you just said in exaggerated voices. "*Pesce* yogurt, *pesce* yogurt, *signora desideri pesce* yogurt. Ha, ha, ha." I don't know what I did but clearly it was a mistake. "*Pesca, signora, pesca* not *pesce.* At least I think that's what you want—peach yogurt? Am I right?" said the nice lady behind the counter, who knew more English than she let on to. "Yes, but isn't that what I asked for?"

"No, *signora*, it's not. And we don't carry fish-flavored yogurt anyway, if that's what you want..."

Finito

ঙIn Tandem

It happens every spring. I come to Naples, Florida, to visit my mother and relax. I didn't realize until this morning, when Mom and I went for our bike ride, that it has become a ritual. She created this practice years ago, and when I visit I enter into it. This is the delicious part for me. I am sharing a private morsel of her morning routine. Something that helps her to feel free and independent. The ability to be physically active without fear of falling.

Previously, Mom had decided to stop riding her bicycle because she no longer felt confident on it. It was my husband's idea to get her the three-wheeler for her eightieth birthday five years ago. I thought it was a terrible idea, sure that she would never get on it because it evoked too many stigmas and images of "old age" and feebleness. I was dead wrong. She was enthusiastic from the day we gave it to her. Once she mastered the awkwardness of steering the two back wheels, she was off and pedaling. Similar to the mailman's creed of not letting rain nor wind keep her from her circuit, she does not miss a day. I believe she really misses it when she comes north to visit all of us.

So, for the ritual. She is ready to bike after she has had her breakfast of juice, coffee, and vitamins, taken her shower and dressed appropriately for the weather. Not at all con-cerned about her looks, she dons one of her most comfortable pair of shorts or pants and some loose-fitting shirt. She prefers to be unencumbered by a bra. We get on our bikes and exit the garage. I get on one of the two-wheelers that she keeps for guests. Slowly we meander out of her cul-de-sac along

Greentree Drive over the bridge to Pelican Bay Boulevard into the Commons where we get on the berm. I always ride behind her because I want to be a buffer if she pulls out and a car comes up too soon and close to her. I also just like to watch her so that I can imprint her image.

Her short, silver-gray hair shines in the sun. Her back has become frail, yet there is strength and a posture of dignity as she sits regally on her bike. It is not easy to ride beside her because she takes up too much curb space, so we don't chat a lot. Instead, we admire the many shorebirds that arrive in the early morning, particularly when the water is high on the berm. There are ibises, a wood stork couple, gallinules, egrets, herons and occasional roseate spoonbills. Every once in a while one of us might make a comment about an anhinga that is drying its wings or an alligator that is making its way up the berm or nesting with her young. At some point on our ride, I will make the sound of a duck, saying "Quack Quack." It is as if I am one of Mom's little chicks following close behind her. I think she gets a kick out of it.

I have also noticed that Mom says "Good Morning" to the kindred early-morning walkers, bikers, and joggers she passes. Some respond and some do not. Some have gotten to know her by her name, "Ninette," and some have even gotten to know my name. I am aware that men often say "Good Morning" to her; when I say "Good Morning" in kind, they respond with a "Hi!" Do I get the "Hi" because they already said "Good Morning" to Mom, or because the term fits a younger person? If they knew that I am in my sixtieth year, would it still be the same?

During one of our rides, I was amused by a comment a little six or seven-year-old redheaded girl made to her sister and to Mom. We were getting off the boardwalk berm as they were entering. She looked at Mom's bike with curiosity and scrutiny and noticed the wire basket in the back filled with rain gear, hat, sweater, gloves, and a warm jacket. Eyeing the basket and then Mom, she said, "Do you have to pull all that laundry?" Mom did not hear her and kept riding. I did and chuckled, saying to myself, "What an original perception." The image of Mary Poppins came to mind.

For me, it is a delightful and tender thing that Mom and I do together. Something that I would not miss for the world. I have come to treasure our forty-five minute amble through the streets of Pelican Bay and on to the boardwalk to see the bird life, the alligators and the flowers and fauna. I hope we have many more years of these silent, special moments together. If not, I will always have the memory of watching my mom from the back as she peddles her way in bliss, and I follow.

ꙮPaula Petersonꙮ

Sweet Memoriesꙮ

My grandfather's name was George Henry Roll. Everyone called him Rollie. He was married to my maternal grandmother, Nina Baekeland, for fourteen years. Banished because of his strong Catholic convictions, as well as preferring a lifestyle of simplicity and order, he found himself divorced but not apart from his large, extended family. He had four children, plus twenty-two grandchildren.

Rollie was a strikingly tall, handsome man. His chiseled, high-cheek-boned face supported a thick mustache and a bald head. It was his hands that fascinated me. They dwarfed a telephone receiver. His gnarly, crooked fingers bent every which way. It didn't seem to stop him from any manual project he was fixed on doing. I can still see him now, whittling with a small pocketknife as he peels and quarters a MacIntosh. I am not sure why, but he never ate the skins of apples or tomatoes.

Winter seemed to be his favorite season. It probably centered around his love of building fires in his log cabin in Redding, Connecticut. When we visited, we were warmly greeted with a crackling fire. He taught my older brother, Jeffrey, the skill of fire making, as well as how to chop and split wood. Methodically, they would stack each log, cord by cord, between two giant oaks. He often wore his signature Scottish wool hat to protect his bald spot.

I looked forward to the times when Rollie visited us in Great Neck on Long Island. There were a few time-honored amusements that my brothers and I would play. One I liked was stepping my bare feet on top of his leather-beaten shoes, as he would hold me just enough so as not to let me fall, and we would dance circles around the room. Another one of our entertainments was huddling around his chair and watching him as he pretended to swallow a tennis ball. Maintaining an element of surprise, we watched it settle in his upper arm, knowing full well that he was flexing his muscle. Laughing and playing along with the gag was the fun part. Rollie was a quiet, thoughtful man who followed a protocol even when he smoked his pipe. After the tamping and lighting, the subtle sweet smell of tobacco was most inviting to be around. He was decisive regarding his likes and dislikes, doing everything in moderation. Just one glass of sherry before dinner, no need to buy more than a sweater or two, and make sure you finish what you have before you go out and get more. He was content to be the armchair traveler, while my grandmother took the flamboyant role of voyaging around the world. Between you and me, that's probably why my grandmother divorced him, along with her intolerance of his wanting to bring his children up Catholic.

I have a delicious recollection of being with him at breakfast. I was about three and too young to go to school, so when my brothers got on the bus I would have Rollie all to myself. He had a habit of eating breakfast that resembled some sort of religious ritual.

I waited for him at the bottom of the stairs to come down and begin his morning practice. He was always showered, shaved and fully dressed, ready to seize the day. "Good morning, Pumpkin," he would say with a smile and then head straight to the kitchen to make his favorite meal. First, he would open the bread box and take out the loaf of dark, heavy-grained bread. He took the serrated knife from the counter drawer, and with his big, gnarly hands he cut two thick slices then popped them in the toaster set at dark. Next, he would pour himself a glass of freshly-squeezed orange juice. My mother made fresh juice every morning, and if she didn't squeeze it herself, one of my brothers would. When I was old enough to stand on a chair and reach the long, curved juicer lever, I helped, too.

The coffee was made. Rollie liked it with milk. When the toast was ready, crisp and very dark, he slowly and methodically spread it with butter. The toast didn't need to be hot because our butter was always soft. We never put it in the fridge, preferring it to paint evenly on any edible surface.

I liked the next part of the ritual the most. He would pick up the teaspoon by his place setting, dig it into the jar of combed honey and take out a big scoop, twisting it so not a drop was wasted. Most of it he drizzled on his toast, but I got to lick the rest. By this time, I am standing nose high to the dining room table, right beside him. I gazed as he paused and savored the moment just before that first taste. Not speaking, simply swallowing a sip of his coffee, he would take a loud, crunching bite out of his toast. Holding the toast towards me, as if to say, "Want a bite?" I shook my head "No" and continued licking the honey off the spoon.

᠙Ex-patriot

Antalya, Turkey—Walked around after our tour of the Archeological Museum, where we saw a near-perfect statue of Artemis with eighteen testes hanging from her chest.

We ended up at a small outdoor restaurant overlooking the Mediterranean. I couldn't wait to have a beer and sit for a spell. After the beer and coffee, we decided to have lunch— baked calamari, salad, grilled vegetables. I had a white wine.

As we ate our lunch, a woman arrived at the adjacent restaurant, only distinguishable by the different-colored tablecloths. She caught my eye and my curiosity. I had watched her as she walked down the promenade toward her restaurant. All in white, gauzy white, expensive white. A loose-fitting top that flowed with her walk and loose-fitting pants as well. Simple leather sandals on her feet. Her hair, cropped to the nape of her neck, was very straight and snow white. Although she did not appear old enough to have white hair, her face did show signs of a life lived hard. It was suntanned a golden brown, yet her telltale profile exposed deep wrinkles and puffy jowls. Her eyes were blue, a soft aqua blue that I imagine would need the protection of sunglasses most of the time— maybe for other reasons, too. Her hands were not unique. Disappointing, in fact. Plain, with short, stubby fingers and bitten nails. No jewelry.

On the promenade just before entering the restaurant, she was greeted by the "barker." They kissed familiarly, and then she sat down next to a portly gentleman—belly, little if any hair. A kiss on his forehead, between them silence. She appeared to be his ornament.

She was handed a tall stemmed glass of chilly white wine almost before she had settled into her appointed seat. Not stirring, she looked out at the sea and the small ships passing in the harbor. She spoke almost not at all, only gazing out. When her wine glass was half full, the bartender appeared from behind the wooden bar, and she was replenished. I imagined that she does this every day. This is her life.

She comes to the bar around noon. *Reposes*. She knows the clientele, the barker and the others who stop by to acknowledge her. Maybe the barker is her son, or maybe her lover or perhaps a gay friend. She is poised in her spot, commanding attention without asking or seeking it out. The bar crowd is family to her, milling about and engaged with each other, drinking slowly until 6:00 p.m.

At 6:00 p.m. they retire to their rooms. I imagine hers to be small, with lots of bed linens of decorative shapes and colors, one on top of another. Very tasteful and exotic. Light fills the room from one large, open, curtainless window. Air stirs throughout the room, which isn't comprised of much more than the bed and pillows of all shapes and sizes. In the corner stands one small, wooden chair with clothes thrown over it so thickly that it is hard to tell what is actually under all the clutter. She naps on top of her bedding, wearing only her lingerie.

The evening begins several hours later at another bar restaurant. Maybe she ends the night in a private room, inhaling warm hashish, alone or not. She is taken in by the night and the darkness. Finally to sleep, only to wake the morning after to do it all over again.

ᦷThe Nature of Grace

In January, my husband, John, surprised me with a long weekend at Skytop Lodge in the Poconos. It was in celebration of my 60th birthday. We had ventured there a decade earlier for my 50th birthday. The afternoon we arrived we took a long walk around the lake on the Skytop property, returning to our room at dusk. Relaxing in our room before dinner, I received a phone call from my middle son, Erik. He and his wife, Kristen, had decided that it would be a good idea to have their daughter's baptism a couple of weeks earlier than had originally been planned. I agreed and understood perfectly. Erik's father, my ex-husband, Aubrey, was in the final weeks of his fight with fourth-stage pancreatic cancer. The substantive concern that he might die before the baptism was not an option. He had to be there with all of us.

Erik and Kristen, in their love and generosity of spirit, had asked Aubrey's wife, Lecia, to be the godmother and John to be the godfather to their daughter Stella. This offer was particularly poignant because neither Lecia nor John has biological children. When John and I married eighteen years ago, I was forty-two. My three sons were grown. This new union was about us and not about raising another family. Aubrey felt the same, although our spouses were disappointed. The announcement that Lecia and John would be made godparents touched everyone.

Aubrey had some ideas of his own regarding Stella's baptism. Previously, when we baptized our three sons, we did it at home, asking a minister to come to us. We resurrected an heirloom silver bowl for the baptismal font. It was engraved and was big enough to hold a honeydew melon, but not an infant. It had originally belonged to Aubrey's grandfather, Captain Andrew Herman, given to him as a prize for his command of the racing schooner *Atlantic* that held the west-to-east record across the North Atlantic from 1905 to 2005. This family award was the central religious piece for our boys' baptisms. This time it would be different. Traditional in every way. It would take place at St. Luke's Episcopal Church in East Hampton, and there would be two ministers presiding. One from St. Luke's and another from the church that Aubrey and Lecia attend in Black Point, Connecticut. This arrangement was very important to Aubrey. No one had any objections to his plans, so the children moved ahead with the organizing.

Setting the date was paramount. Making it a few weeks earlier proved to be problematic for the minister who usually presides at St. Luke's. He was on vacation. When asked, the replacement minister was honored to be part of the baptism and bring Stella into the family of God by purifying her spirit and sanctifying her name. We had less than two weeks to prepare. The date was set for Sunday, January 27, 2008.

Everyone helped coordinate the day. My eldest son, Aubrey, offered to organize and oversee the catering of the brunch, which would be at Aubrey and Lecia's home in East Hampton. I would be the official photographer—a role I have had for almost forty years in our family. My daughter-in-law, Colleen, would prepare the flowers. Other members of the family would secure extra chairs and tables, while others would put out the necessary tableware and glasses with the usual flair and panache that was the order of the day.

As time progressed, so, too, did Aubrey's disease. He was becoming more and more fragile. It was only a few days before the ceremony that he had an additional setback, with an admittance into Southampton Hospital. Another obstruction, coupled with excruciating pain, was a fresh worry. Soon home again and relatively pain free, he was ready and enthusiastic for the big event.

Lecia must have spent a great deal of time thinking about what gift she wanted to give Stella. I know John thought about it a lot. He finally decided on a little butterfly that was set with diamonds and colored precious stones. It hung from a necklace just the right length for Stella. John, however, still wanted to give her more. What would it be? He remembered the good-luck charm of the horn or *"cornicello"* given to children in Italy. We searched the internet and found the perfect one—solid 18-karat gold and only three-quarters of an inch long. It could be worn with the butterfly or on its own. Lecia decided on a very significant baby spoon and pin that had belonged to her mother. The godparents were as excited as new parents.

The day arrived. We assembled at St. Luke's fifteen minutes prior to the beginning of the 10:00 a.m. service. The baptism would take place in the middle of the service, right after the sermon. We were ushered into the first two pews on the left. When it was time for Stella to be christened, the family rose and walked up the nave towards the front of the church. It felt awkward to walk past the congregants, but the font was close to the front doors and on the north aisle. It was stationary. There was no option about where we stood. For the congregants who wanted to watch the process, they had either to turn completely around or, a less desirable option, twist their necks to see and hear what was happening.

Stella looked angelic in her crisp, white christening dress as Erik carried her up to the font and handed her over to Lecia. Her baptism dress had been purchased by her grandmother, Sophie, in Manhattan just days before driving out to East Hampton from Canton, Ohio. It was elegant yet simple. Very much in keeping with the order of the day.

One of the ministers asked Lecia to relinquish Stella into his hands. He solemnly held her up a moment while expressing words to sanctify her soul. He then slowly and gently placed the holy water from the font on her forehead, saying, "in the name of the Lord, I baptize you Stella Sophia Peterson." Stella cried. I've heard it's a good omen. It seemed to me that the entire observance took only minutes before we had to march back to our assigned benches. Albeit brief, it was done with aplomb, and "Bravo!" to Stella.

Family members took turns holding and amusing Stella for the rest of the service. Towards the close of the church service, and after the Eucharistic prayer, there was a pregnant moment when the choir sang "The Lord's Prayer." Had a pin dropped, you would have heard it. It has always been one of my favorite pieces of music, and this particular singing must have captivated everyone, just as it did me.

At that breath, that instant, a shudder ran through my body. Tears filled my eyes and rolled down my cheeks. As if a dam had burst, I had little control of the immense pressure I was experiencing. I knew the truth of it: that the next time I was to grace St. Luke's Episcopal Church it would be to honor Aubrey at his own funeral. Two weeks to the day, he made his transition on Sunday, February 10.

The memorial service was six days later.

"It is the nature of grace always to fill spaces that have been empty."

— Goethe

❧Chef's Helper

My son sets a couple of cloves of garlic and a fat onion on our thick, scuffed cutting board. Deftly slapping the broad side of a six-inch chef's knife hard against the cloves, Luke easily peels off their brown, papery skins. Next, he rhythmically rocks the knife's back half up and down over the cloves, never letting its front end leave the board. In an instant the cloves are impeccably diced. I watch him from my perch, a wicker stool a couple of feet away at the kitchen island. He starts on the onion. In no time, diced pieces, perfectly even, tumble on the board. If it had been left to me, I'd still be working on the garlic.

Feelings are coursing through me, emotions so out of proportion to this simple scene that I have to laugh at myself. I know I'm not watching brain surgery or a master carpenter shaping fine furniture. I know, really, that not much more is going on here than a mother cooking dinner with her twenty-seven-year-old son. But I can't help being mesmerized by his chopping, so economical and quick and controlled. I am charmed, too, by his natural grace as he moves about my kitchen. I am lucky to be cooking with my son. Unmarried, he has moved back home to live with his parents. To some he's a statistic, a reluctant member of a new and burgeoning demographic. Not, of course, to me.

Luke's a busy guy. If he'd had no patience for cooking with his mother, I'd have understood. But he seems content, helping to cook our family meal. He's pitched in willingly, and I admire his dignity, how he's managed to be so clearly adult in a setting that would have had some regressing. It still seems fresh, the fact of his adulthood—even though he was always a mature sort of kid, and I should have been prepared. I savor working alongside him, slowing down my own prep as he maintains speed—I don't want the spell to end. I'm treasuring this fragile moment because I'm sure it won't last. Life will draw him away (as it should, of course), and cooking here won't be so easily arranged.

Some cod is sautéing on my clunky old Garland stove, a stove as old as Luke. I wonder aloud if the fish is ready, and he slips over to check. Luke presses his fingers lightly on the glistening white flesh, saying the fish needs a couple more minutes. I tell him that I would have had to cut into the cod to judge its doneness. He doesn't say anything, but his smile tells me he feels good about his skill. I love his confidence. He wasn't always so self-assured. Once or twice recently he has even veered toward cockiness, tickling me no end. When he disdains my dull knives, the foolish design of my useless kitchen tongs, my failure to buy a blender, I accept the gentle criticism with secret satisfaction. His culinary ballet is a pleasure to watch, that synergy of knowledge, form, and speed. I know he is competent at the restaurant where he cooks, and I hope they appreciate him.

Dinner is almost done—southeast Asian style cod with a beet salad—and I'm getting in the way in my own kitchen, slowing things down. The first time that happened, a Thanksgiving a few years ago, I was astonished. I quit the kitchen and settled on the living room sofa, thrilled as I realized I had passed my sell-by date. Luke speedily made sauces for the vegetables, finished the gravy and mashed potatoes, loaded up the serving dishes, and brought everything into the dining room. I was comfortably sidelined as he took on my old role expertly. It was the natural order of things, and I knew it presaged a lot more than dinner.

✎Jane Andrews✍

✎Winter Sport

My dog, Billy, skitters down the dirt ramp, lowering out of sight as he reaches the water's edge. It is nearly four o'clock, and we are late for our walk. I'd been moping, alone in the house and listless after the bonhomie of the holidays. I knew my mood was plummeting. It does every year as dull January days grip my spirit. I'd had to push myself out of the house, hoping a walk with my dog, even a short one, could short circuit this seasonal sadness. Hurrying to catch up with him, I check to either side. A pair of feisty swans usually lurks in the tall phragmites to the left, finding privacy in the barren stretch of beach that runs behind them. There've been a few face-offs over the years, Billy eventually retreating in response to my plaintive cries. But the grasses are deserted. To the right, the piling from the old dock destroyed during the icy winter of '05 stands sentinel over this corner of Middle Pond. The piling is bare. Usually a cormorant perches on its top, that dark, sharply outlined bird never seeming more than a silhouette as it poses. Will it be spring before it returns?

Across the pond, which glimmers in the weak January light, seasonal cottages stand dark, their owners gone till Memorial Day. The pond's whole shoreline is deserted, save for Billy and me. Strong winds, twenty-five or thirty miles an hour, churn the stainless water, the only movement anywhere. I can hear the ocean's rumble pouring over Meadow Lane and through the Inlet. Sometimes I have had to stop and listen carefully, trying to decide whether I am hearing ocean or wind or the nearby highway. I have no doubts this time. The ocean's bawl powerful enough to be frightening. I call to Billy, looking for reassurance.

Something moves in the air, focusing my eyes. A scarlet streak, long, curved, and hustling high, skims through the steely sky. It flies just on the other side of the stretched, skinny spit of land that leads from Middle Pond to tiny Honey Pot Pond, a sad excuse of a pond, a brackish comma that juts west from the mother pond, depending for its life on high tide. I'd grounded there once in my kayak, so I know just how shallow it is. Only a real estate agent would call this excrescence a pond. This zooming curve, no thicker than a nascent crescent moon, whizzes high, back and forth above the length of the bushy spit. What in the world is it? Without warning the phenomenon suddenly dashes out over the big pond, in full view finally, powerfully rising and falling in its heady run. Caught by its mystery and power, I breathlessly soar with it.

Suddenly my reverie collapses, as my eyes drop from the sky to the water below. A man is skiing furiously on the water, hanging from a rope I can now discern, a taut rope that drops from the mysterious crescent above. Seconds later a gust of wind lifts whoever it is high above the pond's surface. He flies briefly, only to fall gracefully back to the water and zoom along its meniscus, before surging upwards once again. His falls are as grand and elegant as his ascents, as he smoothly swoops through the air down to the water for some glorious skiing back. His movements are so graceful and strong, his presence so unexpected and thrilling, that I resist thinking there is an earthly explanation for all I've seen. For all I know, he might be one of those Greek gods good at speed, the flying Hermes, say, with his winged feet, or Artemis, the fabled runner. Is he as astounded as I that a mere strip of crimson — is it nylon? — buoys him so effortlessly on the wind and water? How he must glory in his mastery of the elements. Does he feel himself to be the center of everything? Does he — can he — know he is a spark promising life in a cold, comfortless landscape? I'm certain he can't see me, and I don't want him to. This radiant moment is private. I call Billy and turn to stroll back to the house, but not before I see the flyer's final fillip over Middle Pond before he is hidden by the shoreline.

❧Jane Andrews❧

Smelling Dirt * ❧

I am in my kitchen smelling dirt. Three new plants—a white kalanchoe and two red begonias—sit on a wrought-iron stand at my window. It is April, five years ago, and I have bought them because it is finally spring. I admire the colors and shapes of their small but dense flowers and their green, waxy leaves. They brighten a neglected corner of my Westchester kitchen. But I hadn't planned on their powerful, raw smell. Working around the house, I try to think about something else. Going upstairs to make beds, the smell follows me, earthy, pushy, almost wet. Perplexed, I wonder how it is that I can smell three small houseplants on the floor below. These aren't even plants known for their fragrance. That afternoon, driving to the grocery store, I still can't shake their dank, ubiquitous odor. Why do I keep smelling them? Could the smell somehow have insinuated itself into my clothes? A day later, twenty miles away at my doctor's office in Manhattan, I am shocked that her office smells, too. But she has no potted plants. And my clothes could not be at fault—running late, I had dressed quickly in fresh clothes, never even going into my kitchen.

    I finally get it. This assertive smell, my uninvited companion for almost two days, is inside my head, not out. Mortified, I think *I* must smell. Talking to friends over the next week or two, I cover my mouth with my hand. I brush my teeth more often, swish mouthwash frequently. But my husband assures me that I smell fine—no bad breath. I finally call my doctor.

---

* A version of this piece was published in *The New York Times*, August 11, 2009.

Dysosmia, I discover, is the name of the medical condition I suffer. *Osmia*, from the Greek *osme*, means "smell," and *"dys,"* also a Greek borrowing, signifies "ill" or "bad" — together they refer to an abnormal or distorted sense of smell. In my case, not just distorting some odorant's smell but, more bizarrely, experiencing a smell when no odorant is present. My exhaustive searches on medical sites online introduced me to another new word that is perhaps even more apt: *"phantosmia,"* a phantom sense of smell. Naturally, medical tests followed. First, I had an MRI of my brain (looking for brain tumors), then a CAT scan of my sinuses (looking for infection), and finally, many months later, an EEG (looking for abnormal brain activity). Since test results were always negative, two rounds of antibiotics (was there some hidden nasal or sinus infection?) constituted my only - and fruitless — treatment.

The earthy smell stuck with me for more than a year until one day I realized that it was finally gone. But to my dismay a new smell immediately took its place. My husband had made a big pot of chili, and he burned it. A pungent odor filled the kitchen. Imprinted with this new odor, I smelled burned chili everywhere, my new default smell. At least it smelled better than dirt. Then, about four years ago, my trip to Provence wiped out the chili. Lavender wafted in the air I breathed, becoming my new smell *du jour*. Southern France's lavender-infested landscape — its dried bouquets, scented soaps and candles, even flavorings for food — trailed me back to the States. Some might think me lucky — lavender's hugely popular. But I hated this smell that had squirmed its way to my poor brain's vulnerable olfactory bulb.

Sufferers from tinnitus or traffic noise play white sound when they want to hear something else. Similarly, I tried to fool my nose. But holding lemons under my nose didn't kill the odor. Smearing pungent perfumes and lotions on my face around my nose didn't work either. Nor did taping my face with gauze pads soaked with these sweet-smelling potions. It's true something powerful like ammonia might hide the lavender for a moment—but there's no cure in that.

Some three years ago relief from lavender came as the smell shifted during my trip to China. My eyes stung and teared and my nose ran as I visited Beijing and Shanghai and some smaller Chinese cities; air pollution was rampant. Flying home, I realized I was still smelling burned coal, factory effluent, and whatever else made up the Chinese air. This new smell was not an improvement on burned chili, and I wasn't sorry to see it leave some four months later.

I can't identify what I've been smelling these last couple of years. The smells have varied, but not a lot. Some have been stronger than others. Occasionally, there have been no disagreeable smells at all. What's new is that the smells usually lack referents in the outside world. Hints of ammonia in their pungency, but definitely not ammonia; wisps of jungle in their smarminess, but yet not jungle; touches of paper factory in their assertiveness, but not quite that awful paper factory smell. Like those describing wine, I invent a potpourri of analogies.

These more recent odors, by now with me only about half the time (there has been improvement), are unsettling in their unidentifiableness. At least when I smelled burned chili, I knew chili was out there somewhere. When pollution odors filled my nose, I remembered those smog-ridden cities in China. When I sniff my current guests, I can't connect them to the real world and face the weirdness of perceiving what is not there—perhaps not unlike a phantom limb.

At times I can't tell where a particular smell is coming from—inside or outside my head. Walking my dog, for instance, I cried as I smelled manure, convinced it was the next new smell in my head. I felt wretched. As I reached home, I rejoiced that the smell was gone. The following day, again while I was walking my dog, the horrid smell reappeared at the same spot. This time I noticed the warning sign: gardeners had spread fertilizer. Only then could I be sure that I was smelling something real.

When my dysosmia returns unannounced — after taking a vacation of a few hours as most days it now does — I am the most distraught. That moment when I first realize the noxious odor is back is especially jolting (since there's no actual odorant, there can be no advertising of its return and no way to prepare for it). I might be chatting with friends over a great dinner or daydreaming in my garden, comfy in an Adirondack chair, when suddenly dysosmia, that pushy partner of mine, arrives head-on.

I try to make clear to my dysosmia just who is in charge. Avoiding gruesome odors is my first line of defense. If I can stop some smell in its tracks, I can win a point or two. There's a coffee shop nearby, for instance, that I simply won't enter. It's jam-packed with huge, rustic, wooden vats of reeking coffee beans that locals complain they smell blocks away. When my husband and I are on a coffee run, I send him inside to buy the coffee while I wait in the car with the windows up. No point in getting imprinted if I can prevent it. (Of course, I've tried the opposite tactic, going out of my way to imprint perfumes, flowers, bakeries, and the like. It hasn't worked. My dysosmia specializes, sadly, in disagreeable odors only.)

Mainly, though, I defend against this militant malady simply by outflanking it. I think right past the dysosmia, ignoring it, forcing my attention elsewhere. If this doesn't work, I laugh at it instead, imagining dysosmia as absurd rather than awful. In this way I try to control the un-controllable. More often than you would think, I succeed, winning a good many of these battles against my affliction. And, with an eye to the future I hope these strategies are preparing me to fight all the other ailments life no doubt has in store for me.

This disorder of mine is best kept private. Since nobody but otolaryngologists have encountered dysosmia, lay people squirm when they confront my uncategorizeable affliction. They suspect some exotic mental disorder. They're not the only ones. I fidget, too. I wonder what it means to hallucinate smell. Perhaps it really is just some killing off of neurons in my olfactory bulb, a primitive part of the brain. Such neuronal deaths might have been caused years ago by a simple cold. But such a hypothesis (proffered by both my latest ENT and by my family doctor) does not deal with my ontological problem. If to you there's nothing plainer than the nose on my face, to me there's nothing more mysterious.

∽Geri Chrein∾

∽The Red Gingham Chair

I noticed it happening slowly over the last year. I have been stepping out of my much cherished comfort zone to do some risky things. On a recent vacation to Puerto Vallarta, Mexico, I found myself and my husband zip-lining through the high jungle canopy. Not only was I surprised by my adventurous choice of venue, my husband was shocked. He continued to glare at me as the bouncy, young Mexican guides collected all our valuable possessions in a communal garbage bag and proceeded to outfit us with hard yellow plastic helmets, V-shaped harnesses that went under our respective crotches and up through our shoulders and thick brown leather gloves for our right hands. In a very brief lecture that assumed we were all born "zipping," they explained how to use our equipment to safely zip through the rainforest on a pulley suspended on cables starting at thirty feet above solid ground. They did show us how to use the glove to squeeze the cable when we wanted to slow down or stop, but initially my natural instinct was to stop immediately when I looked down. We zipped through those trees from platform to platform about ten times and finally rappelled to safety, only to then climb a steep precipice to reach our belongings, the free treat and cold water at the snack bar. Although I laughed for the two interminable hours it took us to reach safety, it was out of fear and discomfort, not joy. We were so stunned by our adventure that we bought the video tape for a reality check. Of course they made a video tape; it was a tourist experience.

Three weeks ago, on a very cold and damp Sunday morning back in Southampton, I went on an early morning "seal walk." On a typical Sunday morning I am very delighted to get up late and slowly make my way down to the kitchen where I read *The New York Times* while having a large cup of coffee with an "everything" bagel. After carefully following the directions I got over the phone, I finally found the parking lot on Westhampton Beach where I was surprised to meet a large group of eager seal watchers. Our enthusiastic guide gathered the group, told us about the seals we could expect to see, but he wasn't making any promises. We didn't see any seals that Sunday, but we did get wet and chilled as we walked for several miles hoping to see just one seal. Either the seals were smarter than we and were in a warm dry spot reading *The New York Times*, or they had departed the Hamptons earlier than usual.

Last week I left my comfort zone again to take voluntarily three classes at the local library: yoga, personal essay writing and tap dancing. I like yoga. It is relaxing and slow, so it fits my personality and age. I also like to write in my comfort zone, which is a personal journal never seen by human or any other eyes. Even I don't read my journal. However, I do fantasize that the world might be a better place and I a better person if I could share my thoughts. And tap dancing, now that is a distorted fantasy for me, a woman who finds it difficult to walk. I spent my first class tripping over my feet and at least two beats behind everyone else. I blamed it on my sneakers and ordered tap shoes as soon as I got home.

What am I thinking? My comfort zone is a red gingham chair in my house in Southampton, New York. My chair faces a wide expanse of glass doors that open to Davis Creek, a tidal creek off Little Peconic Bay. In my chair I am an observer of time and life passing productively. I see ducks, geese, swans, egrets, seagulls and osprey actively living their lives in and around the creek: feeding at dusk, playing mating games in spring and fighting others of their species for territorial rights. I am audience to beautiful light shows: gray, cold days with purple sunsets in winter; clear days with deep blue skies and red, orange sunsets in summer. Every day is different. Every season is outstanding from the abundance of spring to the bareness of winter. The bucolic world I see from my red gingham chair has delighted me for years. At first, when I was working, it became my weekend treat. Later, when I retired, it became a daily treat. Three years ago when I was diagnosed and treated for breast cancer, it became a retreat, the comfort zone that helped me block out all mental, physical and emotional pain and I healed. Last year when I thought the cancer had returned, it became a refuge. After the surgery for what turned out to be a benign adrenal tumor, I again healed in my red gingham chair.

I am not only a passive observer in my red gingham chair, I read many good books by literary and lousy writers. I read thousands of home design magazines searching for gorgeous ideas and guidance to renovate my house and city apartment. I find hundreds of workable and easy recipes to feed me, my husband and visiting family and friends. I read at my own pace, which includes plenty of time for naps. Cooking is not risky for me since it is an "old trick" I learned from my mother. Design and decoration are more risky, but I am a sucker for those beautiful pictures. I was indeed an enthusiastic lifelong learner before I left the comfort and safety of my chair.

Why am I spending less time in the nurturing red gingham chair to take risks that leave me feeling vulnerable? Perhaps I am feeling better and lucky to be alive. I have more energy and time now that I spend less time with doctors. I have been emancipated from their control to my own "recognizance." I am finally ready to be an active participant rather than a passive observer of life. I want my time to be as purposeful and productive as that of the waterfowl on the creek. I have accepted the inevitability of death, and now it is time to accept life. When I completed radiation therapy, a friend asked if cancer had changed me. It was too soon for me to feel changed. I certainly didn't have an epiphany worthy of a Sunday night movie. Now, after some time has passed, I do feel different. It is still not the stuff of miraculous self-revelation, but I do feel open to new experiences, ideas and skills. Will I learn to tap dance? Will I ever learn to write easily and share my writing? Will I ever be able to balance on one foot? Will I ever lose the fear of failure? I don't know, but I am willing to be a bit uncomfortable to find out. Even if I never go zip-lining again, I came away knowing how to use that leather glove to control my zip speed. It took many awkward, twisted zips until I finally "got it," but I was better at the last zips than the first and I have the video to prove it.

ৎGeri Chreinৎ

ৎWhat I Did on My Summer Vacation

I begin with a confession of what I didn't do on my summer vacation. I didn't write one structured or unstructured meaningful essay, paragraph or sentence. I wrote in my journal a few times mainly to complain about not writing, as if confession would absolve me or justify my procrastination. I really do like to write. I am one with William Makepeace Thackeray who said, "You never know what lies within you until you write." I delight in this process of discovery. However, writing is also a serious form of thinking, hard work and a major time commitment. The type of work I usually do from September until June, but never in July and August. Deep in my old head is a child brain that believes that summer is free space, a vacation space. It is the time to collect that symbolic $200; take a deep breath; spontaneously putter about and generally seek comfort, rest and relaxation with a healthy dose of sunshine.

I became a teacher for three main reasons: July, August and my sincere need for people to listen to me. In July and August I willingly gave up my audience to head for the cool outdoor pleasures of the country or beach. Summer is the time for this city girl to connect spiritually to her joyous rural roots. Although I am a born and bred "city girl," these roots go directly into the Catskill Mountains and perhaps reach all the way back to a small village in Russia.

My first ten childhood summers were spent at a *Kuchalein* in the Catskill Mountains. At the end of each school year, the last week in June, my parents would pack a trunk and several boxes to move them and my younger brother Barry and myself from the city (Brooklyn) to the country where we could see not only that one tree, but forests full of trees, acres of green grass and breathe real fresh air. We didn't own a car so my parents hired a "hack" (taxi), which came for us early in the morning as the sun was rising. The driver and my dad would load us and our stuff into this very large black car. Then we would make at least two more stops to load other families going in the same direction. After six hours and one stop at the Red Apple Rest for lunch, we reached our destination and home for the next two months: Uncle Bob's Rooming House in Mountaindale, New York.

Uncle Bob was really my uncle. He was my grandfather's younger brother. After his incarceration for simple car theft, he married Aunt Lil who inherited this aging property of two large stucco houses and a general store from her mother. Uncle Bob and Aunt Lil had one child, the evil Cora.

They converted these two old houses into a fifteen-room Kuchalein, which means to cook by yourself. This is different from a hotel where the rich people vacationed. In a hotel they cooked all your meals for you and offered facilities and planned activities like tennis or handball and a lovely pool. In a Kuchalein you got none of these amenities, but you did get a room large enough for the whole family with a bathroom down the hall; a spot at the stove and a table in the communal kitchen you shared with the fourteen other families.

All activities for children and adults were self-generated and limited only by your needs and/or your imagination. In a Kuchalein you were on your own to create your meals and your entertainment.

My mother talked all summer while she played cards and Mah Jong. She also knitted some sweaters for the winter and prepared meals. My dad and the other men came for weekends and their two-week vacations. He played softball or handball. He and my grandpa would take me for long walks in the fields and the forests where he would explain the natural world to me. Birds sing and fly—grass grows green and naturally—trees have leaves but they are not all the same. Some are oaks and others maple or pine. Aren't we lucky to be here in the clean fresh country air and not in the city? I don't think he really knew much about the natural world, but he and Grandpa knew that they loved it and they were so happy to be here and not in Brooklyn. They were proud that they could take their families to this paradise. For Grandpa it was like the village he left behind in Russia. Both of them loved the freedom of summer in the country on their weekends and two-week vacations. In the country we were rich. We really had the "sun in the morning and the moon at night." That was quite enough and all we really needed.

For us, the children, there was the forest and the brook and, of course, each other. We were mighty adventurers and royalty. Sometimes we were scientists or teachers. We collected salamanders, tadpoles and other muddy specimens from the natural world. We played or hung out all day. Our only obligation was to show up for breakfast, lunch and dinner. We were like lords and ladies of the flies with extremely loose supervision. We were never bored, nor did I ever hear that word used by any child, not even the evil Cora. We never had reading lists and math assignments from school. Somehow, we all passed the tests when September came. Our imaginative play taught us valuable problem solving, artistic and social skills that are rarely part of any school curriculum.

We no longer summer in the Catskill Mountains, although those years set the gold standard for happy, carefree and imaginative summers. As my generation grew up and assimilated more fully into American life, we looked for more diverse and luxurious summer vacations. We sought new adventures in new places. However, summer will forever mean retreat from the city and from all the work and social responsibilities. Summer is when the imagination grows as the mind and body relax. See you in September!

ᔖGeri Chreinᔗ

In the Beginningᔗ

I was wanted and long awaited by both sides of my family: the Eisenbergs, my mother's people, and the Hartmans, my father's people. I would be the first-born child of Rose and Julius Hartman and the first grandchild for both sets of grandparents. Somehow they all hoped a baby would bring them better luck. You see, my parents were married in 1937 during the great depression. Times were hard financially, and politically there was war talk in Europe and Asia. Even though money was scarce Rose and Julie really wanted to have a child, so after two years of a happy marriage they began to try to make that baby...

However, my life began with great difficulty: my mother couldn't become pregnant. If only wanting could make it happen, but no luck, only disappointment, month after frustrating month. I was no accidental pre-boomer; my parents worked and played hard for me. They began to give up the little hope they had of starting a family. The grandparents on both sides, as well as the aunts and uncles, were also discouraged. They offered their advice, which made the couple feel like they were doing something wrong. They also had some silly old-fashioned and superstitious remedies, like eating chickpeas and wearing a red ribbon to ward off evil spirits.

Rabbi Isaacs strongly suggested that Rosie start to visit the ritual bath called the Mikvah. This ritual advises that the couple abstain from sexual relations for fourteen days after the last menstruation and not resume until the wife is cleansed in a ritual bath. All that science knows about human reproduction is embodied in this ancient ritual, but the ancients wept because it didn't help Rosie get pregnant.

Finally, Dr. Nadler, their family physician, recommended that my parents see a doctor who specializes in these matters, a fertility specialist, Dr. Lieberman. My mother was nervous and frightened. Her mother, Sarah, was not only nervous and frightened but offered dire warnings against unnatural processes. Sarah warned Rosie, "If you play with fire you will get burned!" Rosie and Julie went anyway. After a thorough exam of both Mom and Dad, Dr. Lieberman discovered the problem, a blocked fallopian tube, which he skillfully unblocked.

Nine months later at the beginning of May 1941, my mother suffered the longest and most painful labor of any woman thus far in Brooklyn Jewish Hospital or in the recorded history of birthing. As she tells it, she was in the hospital labor room for almost a week. She pushed and she pulled. She screamed and she cursed in both English and Yiddish, but despite her hysteria, I was not ready to make my entrance yet! After about two days she believed that she'd died and went to heaven because she was surrounded by male and female angels dressed in white. She wasn't about to give up her life for mine, and she wasn't about to lose this baby she worked so hard to conceive. So, with almost her last ounce of determination and energy, she saw to it that we both pulled through.

In my mother's rendition of the story, I am not sure where my father is now. I can only imagine, like all fathers in black-and-white movies of that time, he is in a waiting room pacing the floor and chain smoking unfiltered cigarettes. If this is true, then my father is in more danger than my embattled mother as he chain smokes through Rosie's record labor. A labor that is more painful than the depression past and the war to come.

Is my father alone in this waiting room or has the whole family camped out on either side of the path my father needs for adequate pacing? Is his tall brother Mulley pacing with him or his brothers-in-law, Funny Phil and Elegant Harry?

Certainly not skinny, wimpy Sam! I am sure my grandparents Eisenberg and Hartman take turns in the waiting room because they really don't like each other. Neither set of grandparents smokes. When faced with stress like the longest labor in history they eat! I wonder what they eat. Corned beef sandwiches with lots of mustard? Is it on crusty rye bread or club rolls? No! They would save such luxurious food for the bris, since they don't know if Rosie is having a boy or a girl. I am sure they are eating chicken sandwiches on pumpernickel with lots of schmaltz (chicken fat) and salt. If I am correct, they too are in at least as much danger of premature death as is my poor mother!

After this long wait in dangerous conditions of smoke and schmaltz, they get the news that I have finally been born. The doctor, dressed in white hat and smock, enters the waiting room and announces to the exhausted audience, "It is a healthy 9 pound 10 ounce baby girl. Mother and daughter are doing just fine! Despite their temporary disappointment that it is not a boy, they hug and congratulate each other and are thrilled about this new baby girl. Grandpa Hartman, the most generous family member, runs out to the deli for corned beef sandwiches with plenty of mustard for all, even the Eisenbergs.

Meanwhile, in the labor room my mom was coming out of the anesthesia they finally gave her to relieve her suffering and theirs. As Mom looked up she saw one of the angels, an African-American woman named Geraldine—clearly spelled out on her name badge. Geraldine gently wiped my mother's brow as she had done for the past week while my mother was laboring. Mom had grown to love Geraldine and at that exact moment of brow wiping my name changed from Gail to Geraldine. Even though my mom is not poetic by nature, my middle name became Hope. Was it "Hope" for a better economy? Hope to avoid the war? I was soon to find out what she hoped for.

Out of the womb just a short time and so far all seemed to be progressing well. I had a name, an odd name for a Jewish girl born in 1941, but Mom liked unusual names and things. Geraldine Hope was different and would always call attention to me in the schools of East Flatbush, Brooklyn, New York. Lovely as it was I would have preferred Joan, Janice, Marilyn, Alice or the much coveted Susan and Betty.

Into our calm room burst the woman I affectionately would forever call the wicked witch of East Flatbush, Sarah Eisenberg, my maternal grandmother. She certainly had a flair for drama. I couldn't understand everything she was saying. She spoke mostly in Yiddish with grand gestures, flailing arms and tearing eyes and a high-pitched loud voice. All this made her seem much larger than her 4'8". I was always bigger than her, even at birth weighing in at almost ten pounds and measuring 23 inches. I had a full head of black hair and a wrinkled and bruised face. Some would have considered me a miracle, but Sarah was horrified. She didn't run over to kiss Mom and congratulate her. She didn't want to hold me or even touch me. Instead, she cried louder, shouting, "*Oy* mine Rosie, mine Rosie, *Oy* mine Rosie. I nearly died in the waiting room. I was so worried about you. I was so nervous that I couldn't even eat. I nearly fainted. I felt so sick that my heart was running away. I sat there so long that I almost died...." Then her wild eyes went from my mom to the ceiling and landed on me. She let out a blood-curdling scream, which brought the original Geraldine into the room. She then fainted and Geraldine brought her some smelling salts. When she came to, she was as white as my blanket and she said, "*Oy vey! Minah Tsurus! Oy ah suchen vey!*" She spit three times over her left shoulder to ward off the evil spirits and proclaimed for all to hear, "MINE ROSIE HAS GIVEN BIRTH TO A MONKEY!!!!!!!! A MONKEY!!!!!!! *OY VEY!!!!!!!!!!!*.

At this point Rosie seriously thought of sending me back. What a waste of her time and energy. She thought that God might have been telling her something when she couldn't get pregnant. She worried that Dr. Leiberman did something evil to her. Why did she work so hard at conceiving and birthing? The mother she had tried to please so much all of her life was hysterically denouncing her baby as subhuman, a monkey. The baby she hoped was her gift to her husband and family. In truth, she also thought this oversized, hairy baby she had just named Geraldine Hope was, well, "different."

Now I knew where all the "Hope" came from—it wasn't hope for a better economy or world peace—it was hope that this monkey child would eventually turn into the real human child who would make her proud, give her some *nachas* and be loved by all, especially by her mother, the diminutive Sarah.

❧Geri Chrein❧

❧I Am a Shopper

I am a shopper. I confess that when my world seems chaotic and I am stressed out, I go shopping. Some people overeat, others drink and still others seek gratification through internet porn. I simply go shopping, which, by comparison, is a harmless emotional outlet. Shopping is my safe space. Others, like my husband, find no comfort in shopping. They have mild anxiety attacks when shopping for anything more complex than a Band-Aid. They are the anti-shoppers, and I am the shopper. For me shopping is full of hope. Walking through a well-stocked store stirs my imagination. Each potential purchase promises personal comfort and transformation. Within the design, fabric or color of a gorgeous garment or accessory is a world of possibilities. So when I am feeling low and want to feel younger, smarter, or prettier, I shop. Even if I don't buy a thing the ambiance of a fine or fun store elevates my mood with sensual delights. Department stores greet me with lovely music, classical or jazz. They smell of the finest perfumes, and lately many stores have "events" that also come with food and drink.

Are shoppers born ready to hit the stores or are they nurtured into existence? I am the second generation in four generations of outstanding and skilled shoppers. Before me is my now 92-year-old mother, Rosie. After me is my 40-year-old daughter, Jennifer, and after her is her 21-month-old daughter, Jolie, a shopper in training.

Rosie, the elder matriarch of the clan, believes that it is important for a woman to look good in public. She is a first generation American, the daughter of Russian Jewish immigrants. Her father, like most Jewish immigrants who came to America at the turn of the century, went into the garment business. He started and ended his career as a tailor in "cluks and suts," which, as a child, I finally decoded as cloaks and suits. Since he was out of work seasonally, he spent his down time making a limited number of very fine garments for his two daughters. He had the skill, but the material was expensive. Rosie saw looking good as a way to fit in and eventually assimilate into the mainstream culture, and also as a way of looking as good as her many attractive and mostly more affluent female cousins.

When she began to earn her own living as a receptionist in an expensive downtown restaurant called Schlifers, she went shopping in the nearby department stores looking for beautiful yet affordable clothing. She quickly self-trained as a master bargain shopper. As a shopper she was fortunate to be five foot seven inches tall, thin and very attractive, with long black hair and pale ivory skin. She is fond of telling the story of how she was almost discovered by a Zeigfeld scout who saw her at the restaurant. Her career in show biz was immediately cut short when they insisted that she wear a revealing cellophane costume. My mother turned them down, not only for decency and propriety, but for appearances. Now, if they would have offered her a Chanel suit with matching spectator pumps reduced 50% off the original ticket price, my mom might have been a star. Being a show biz star wasn't important to my mom; looking like a star was her goal.

My mom not only loved to shop, she was very good at it. She valued the bargain, and bargains she found. My mother fledged me into the world of shopping with the sincerity of a mother bird teaching her young to fly. She carefully and patiently instructed me in the art and science of shopping. When I was very young we trained at the major downtown Brooklyn department stores: Mays, known for their low prices; A&S and Martins, known for their higher prices but excellent seasonal sales. I learned how to negotiate the racks in department stores by doing the "overlook"—a quick scan of the merchandise to locate the sale signs and hone in on the styles and colors we wanted. She instructed me never to make eye contact with persuasive self-serving salespeople. I learned how to seem disinterested in a prized garment if other women seemed too interested. My disinterest appeared to be rejection of the garment, so they most often backed off, leaving the path clear for Mom and me. I wasn't much good at math in school, but I was a whiz at discounts. I could instantly compute percentages — 10, 20, 40 and the sacred 50% off. It is not widely known but Mom invented the idea of mix and match, knowing we would get the best bargains on a top without a bottom or a bottom without a top. These items were more likely to be marked down. A clever shopper should be able to quickly match stray tops with lonely bottoms or mentally scan her home closet for a possible match. The reward was a cheap, yet unique and often beautiful outfit.

Shopping made Mom happy, and because I displayed such an early aptitude for it, my mom was very proud of me. Even though I liked to play stick ball with the boys, my mom was beginning to believe that I might turn out to be a girl who would look good. I was an honor shopper and the rewards were plentiful. Not only did we find cheap treasures, Mom also treated me to lunch at the upstairs Chinese restaurant. We always sat in the front table near the window and ordered the combination plate, which came with egg drop soup, chicken chow mein, fried rice, egg roll and pistachio ice cream, all for fifty cents. Even that was a bargain. Not only did we get our spiritual sustenance from shopping on Saturday while my father went to Synagogue, we ate forbidden non-kosher Chinese food and really enjoyed it. I think that Mom discovered Chinese food with the "girls" from her Mah Jong group, who would save money to take themselves out to theater and dinner a few times each year.

When I finally grew a bust and started to date, Mom took me to Loehmann's, the holiest of all clothing stores, where every day was a sale day. Designer dresses could be had for as little as ten dollars, and I am talking Evan Picone, the Donna

Karan of the 50s. Before suburban Jews invented the Bat Mitzvah in the 60s, Jewish girls knew they reached womanhood when their moms took them to Loehmann's. It was a temple of gratification for the educated shopper. Imagine a bargain store housed in a two-story brick mansion behind heavy black and gold gates. Inside, it was even more imposing, with its stained glass windows, pink marble floor and a grand marble and gold staircase. The less expensive clothes were on the first floor, and the special designer clothing was on the second floor. With all this grandeur, Loehmann's did not have one dressing room. So we tried on the dresses in public. There was no shame where bargains were concerned. My mom, who turned down fame and fortune because of a theatrical cellophane dress, thought nothing of undressing in public for a real bargain. On a balcony between the first and second levels was a sitting area for dutiful husbands who drove their wives to the store. As their reward they got to see the best and least inhibited strip show in town as all the ladies on the first floor frantically tried on and discarded dresses.

Loehmann's is still a name synonymous with bargains, but it has gone through many incarnations. It is now owned by a major retail chain, and you can find stores all over America. When I really need a major shopping fix I visit the Manhattan store. I buy very little there because the real good stuff seems to come only in small sizes, but even so I feel at home as I wander through the store using all the shopping skills I learned from my mom. Just a few weeks ago I spotted a black Dolce & Gabbana jacket in a size twelve on sale for less than two hundred dollars, and I knew I was a real winner. When my mom needs a shopping fix she asks me what I am giving away. Now that is a real bargain for her and the ultimate compliment for me.

๑Truth or Consequences

I'm standing on a gurney and a woman in a white uniform is taking my shirt off. My five-year-old mind is wondering why this strange woman is undressing me. It seemed just minutes ago Momma dressed me and we left our apartment with Momma saying we're going someplace where I'd play with kids, there'd be swings and I'd get ice cream.

Grandma, who lived on the same apartment building floor, and my fourteen-year-old sister, Bessie, were with us as we made our way along busy Orchard St., with its steady stream of street pushcarts on either curbside, to Broome and then east two blocks to Essex St.

The nurse is now putting my left arm, then my right, through the openings of an open-back gown when another gurney is wheeled into the sterile, windowless room. There is someone lying on her side, and a nurse is holding a white pan inches from her mouth.

The gurney is wheeled closer to mine. I see it's Bessie spitting out blood into the pan. I scream, "BESSIE, BESSIE," but she doesn't move, only globules of darkish red blood gush out of her mouth. She's been KILLED and I'm next to be SLAUGHTERED! I'm strapped down to the gurney as I scream, "NO, NO, PLEASE NO. HELP ME." I feel my gurney being wheeled. The ceiling and its yellowish round lights move backwards slowly, rapidly, into a dizzying stream. I flash back.

Bessie is sitting on the living room floor doing her homework. I move her notebook for attention. She gets annoyed, says "stop it," and resumes writing. After a moment, I impishly take her book. Bessie screams, "I told you stop it," takes back her book, gets up, turns her back to me and says angrily, "You're bad, I don't like you" as she walks away.

I yell ragefully, "No. No," and run after Bessie with my right, raised fist. Bessie runs into the kitchen, past Momma at the sink, and into the bedroom, slamming the door behind her. I run up to the closed door, swing wildly, hitting a glass square panel that breaks into flying pieces. Momma, upset that I woke up Poppa sleeping in the bedroom before he goes to work the night shift, angrily yells at me, "Nowa yua wokka upa Poppa, nowa yua gonna get it."

The gurney stops directly below a bright white ceiling light. A shadowed, masked face appears. I yell for my life, "NO, NO, PLEASE, PLEASE, DON"T KILL ME." The voice commands me to count to ten. I see a black, round death mask aimed at me, quickly enlarge, then it's over my face. I slowly count 1--2----3------4--------5----------6------------.

We are now walking on Essex St. toward Delancey. Momma, in a contrite voice, says something about tonsils and how awful she felt hearing me scream "help" as she walked down the stairs and into the dispensary lobby waiting area.

We enter Levi's Hot Dogs and Knishes on the corner. Momma orders my favorite vanilla custard and hands it to me. "Here, Gianni, itsa gonna maka yua feella betta."

My hands don't move, my arms and legs stiffen, I'm still strapped to the gurney. I don't dare open my mouth; I turn my head away.

᭙Brother Danny

It was one of those hot, humid July nights when the concrete sidewalks and asphalt streets started to breathe some relief from the day's sweltering heat. Danny Petrale and I were walking home on Delancey St., having just treated ourselves to potato pirogies at Ratner's, an air-conditioned oasis. It, or another Lower East Side eatery like Katz's Deli, was often our reward after classes at Washington Irving night high school.

We both hated our jobs. I was a 27-year-old who dropped out of school at 16, working at a job polishing jewelry with dirty compounds in a sixth-floor shop on Canal St. Danny, several years younger, also a drop-out, would take his school books home, perhaps make a sandwich to take with him to the financial district to work the night shift, feeding behemoth-sized computers data cards with holes in them.

We met in night school and eventually became good friends. I wouldn't realize until many years later that Danny was just what I needed to make my transition at a critical time when I was uprooted from family, friends and a lifestyle I was attempting to escape.

I'd been in many a barroom fight or on the streets turned mean over girls, turf, a slight or stupid remark fed by alcohol and settled with explosions of broken bottles, knives, bats, lug wrenches, a car chase to run someone down on the sidewalk, and, inches from me, a killing.

Weeks before I registered for night school, my life was threatened in a bar by a Mafia-type from Mulberry Street in Little Italy. A friend had been killed around that time in his building hallway late one night.

After the barroom threat, walking home alone when the streets were empty and my hallway dimly lit, I'd imagine that out of the shadows would emerge a figure, the fire of a gun.

Now Danny was a different kind of tough guy. A Hero. An ex-marine football player who looked the part, amplified with a bellowing, booming voice. And there was more. Danny was a Christian evangelist who preached with his mother on the New York City sidewalks and at a storefront church his mom founded in "Alphabet City" (Avenues B, C, D) on the Lower East Side.

When I was most vulnerable, with my defenses weakened, I felt safe with Danny. That July night as we ambled along the Delancey St. sidewalk, we heard the screeching of two car tires coming to a halt, then yelling, curses, threats of rageful young men alongside their cars parallel to us. We watched the flailing arms and contorted bodies move onto the sidewalk about fifty feet in front of us. One man, the target, was knocked down and the others started kicking him repeatedly, looking like a barracuda pack. Another with a lug wrench in his raised hand approached for the killing. My stomach tightened and my body froze at the too often familiar unfolding scene.

Danny shoved his books into my midsection, like they were a football, saying, "Hold this," as he took off running toward the pack with all his might. When he was about five feet from them, he threw his 240-pound solid frame into a flying tackle and knocked down every one like bowling pins. As he started to raise himself to one knee, he yelled with his huge voice, "GET OUT OF HERE," and they disappeared like rodents in a flash, fearing another lightning bolt.

I ran behind Danny after a moment of shock. But besides my shock I hesitated; yes, we were outnumbered, but I heard a primal voice: act only, especially if there's danger, if it's your tribe. I was not yet part of Danny's tribe, nor were the fighting strangers.

I clutched our books as I got to him, virtually speechless and amazed at what I had just witnessed, and finally stammered, "You saved that guy's life."

Danny thanked me for being there with him as he took his books with a dismissive shrug of the shoulder, implying what he did wasn't anything out of the ordinary. It was as if "he was his Brother's Keeper."

Shortly after, I witnessed Danny with amazing speed and skill save another stranger's life from suicide. On another late night, a woman ran out of a building on Rivington St., hysterical. "Help. Help, somebody, my husband killed himself." She ran desperately to us, the only ones on the street. "He swallowed a bottle of pills." We asked where and ran up a flight of stairs before her to the open-wide apartment door to the kitchen. A man's body sprawled face down on the dull bluish kitchen linoleum with a blurred pattern, between the white sink and pink Formica table and a cheap chrome-plated legged chair. A round fluorescent ceiling lamp bleakly lit the scene and the ghastly pallor of the man's skin. He wore only gray boxer shorts and a white sleeveless tank undershirt. An empty pill bottle lay on the floor beside his head.

Danny quickly crouched to one knee, turned the man like a doll, face up, cradled his head to pull open an eyelid, and shouted, "Laundry detergent, get some detergent and a cup." The wife got a box from a cabinet and I found a cup on the sink drainboard. Danny dashed to the sink, mixed water with the detergent, and, back on one knee, raised the comatose body to a sitting position, then lowered the head as he emptied the concoction down his throat.

Within seconds the man vomited, grimaced, and opened his eyes. His wife, seeing him come alive, hit his arm, slapped his face, then the arm again and again, screaming, "You bastard. How could you do this?" Then, getting down to her knees, she cried as she hugged him, pleading, "Don't do this to me again." He, in a stupor, could not or would not respond, kept his chin down to his chest as we lifted him to the chair.

She thanked us, mumbling something about his gambling and losing everything as we left.

About ten years later, I was close to graduating college and I wanted to "give something back," believing I was lucky. "Somebody upstairs" had looked after me. I had volunteered for a Quaker project working with the homeless on The Bowery. One bitter-cold, windy night, the temperature in single digits, four of us volunteers walked along The Bowery. We saw a dark-skinned man with a trimmed mustache, perhaps in his forties, lying unconscious on the sidewalk. A strong smell of alcohol and the overpowering stench of urine were evident as we examined him to see if he was injured or perhaps had a heart attack. After reviving him enough to answer a few questions, it was clear he did not need an ambulance. However, we told him he needed to get out of the cold, that he was in danger of losing fingers or toes to frostbite or worse.

The man tacitly agreed to go to the City Men's Shelter four blocks away. However, when we lifted him up, he was unable to stand on his own. We agreed we'd straddle him over our shoulders. I put one of his arms around my shoulders as did another volunteer around his, the man's arms stretched out and his head hung to the side as if he was on a mobile cross, feet barely touching the sidewalk.

The sharp cocktail stench of urine, vomit and alcohol, and the sight of his soiled pants and jacket, were nauseating and repulsive. Yet, the Quaker philosophy that there is "god within everyone" enabled me to see the Light in this crucified stranger and gave me the strength with each labored step forward to the shelter.

It was then I realized that my "tribe had grown wider." Thank you, Brother Danny: No Greater Gift Hath Been Given.

❧My Gracious Friend

We met by odd chance almost twenty years ago: you, the separated husband; I, the latest beau, sitting in what was likely your favorite, softly cushioned den chair in your most stunning home on the wetlands on Accabonac Harbor. You came looking for one of your tools to fix something at the rental you lived in with your eldest son, Aubrey.

Paula, still your wife, introduced us and you extended your warm, welcoming handshake with the smile of the host, as if you were still living in your home. I recoiled inwardly, felt like a thief, wanting to escape up the den fireplace, and extended my hand tentatively. I imagined your pain but you showed no sign of it, just a warm welcome, except perhaps for a hint of alcohol on your breath.

You, tall, thin, a handsome WASP, a look-alike for George Bush, the elder, or Jimmy Stewart, a product of Exeter, Yale and the upper class. I, the short, high school drop-out, who finally finished City College after years of night school, from the Lower East Side and of Sicilian, working-class, immigrant parents. I felt out of my league.

Over these almost twenty years we've known each other, I've grown so fond of you. We fussed over the Yankee/Mets/Red Sox rivalries, betted lunch on the World Series. You got to root for the underdog to be a Mets/Red Sox fan; and we've delighted talking about the Metropolitan Opera performances. Oh, do I envy your subscriptions to the Metropolitan Opera year after year.

And the boys. You so generously shared with me your greatest treasure: your loving, exceptional, handsome, tall, accepting-of-me three sons. They so eased my anxious, yet joyous, journey as their step-dad. Undoubtedly, like father, like sons, they got so much of their emotional intelligence from you.

At first I thought the boys would resent me, the interloper, and never accept that "I took" their mom away from them and from you when I married her. I thought Oliver, the youngest, needed a strong, attentive and loving step-dad who showed him the value of a close-knit family and proper discipline. That intention, although loving, was a joke, since I never was a parent before and he already had a dad. I imagined the divorce affected him badly; he did seem uprooted and raged at times.

How wrong I was. You were all he wanted and needed. He was very angry about the divorce. Yet you were always there for him: supportive, yet with tough love when that's what he most needed.

What grand, proud celebrations we've had at their graduations. The one in Buffalo was so exciting; we took in the Maid of the Mist boat ride in Niagara Falls. Rehearsal dinners, three wonderful weddings, the blessed christening of a grandson, another pregnancy, and now the blessing of a granddaughter. Then there was the deep pain of what was a life-threatening crisis of one of the boys; that chapter has had a happy ending!

When I talk to the boys, I will at times refer to you as "Dad" instead of "your dad." It seems I want to have no separation from the boys and from you.

You've been diagnosed with a life-threatening disease, fourth stage pancreatic cancer. You appear to be accepting of it, doing all you can, and your attitude suggests you'll enjoy the time and life you have left the best way possible.

I am not so accepting. I pray every morning for your healing, for you to be alive a long time. I recently lit a candle in a church in Quebec City. I know it's an irrational feeling of loss. At first I felt guilty it wasn't me, because I'm older than you are and it would be less painful for the boys. I want to do more, something, but don't know what. You have been so generous to me and I've been the fortunate one of your bounty.

When I married Paula I felt loved, whole and blessed. The boys' acceptance of me and their relationship was part of the fringe-benefits package, and a new, happy journey opened up for me. You are part of my journey, and the boys are a big part of you.

I'm feeling separation anxiety, loss; I want to scream, "Please don't go gently into the night." How can you be so accepting!

Cancer ripped my precious, gentle brother from my heart at 64. It stole my two strong, handsome, loving uncles in their prime.

My mother, sister, dad, aunt, cousin, friends survived it.

Can't you? Please God.

❧John Tusa❧

I Love My Honda❧

I don't say "I love you" easily. Just ask my wife. We've been together more than twenty years. And I'm better at saying "I love you" to Paula, paradoxically, the more I've grown secure and vulnerable in our marriage of 19 years. Before then, if I ever said "I love you" to a girlfriend, it was once at the start of a relationship, as "My Declaration of Codependence," or as it was ending, then I'd feel my codependency scream, "I love you, DON'T LEAVE ME!"

From the first day I bought you, my black, shiny, 1996 two-door, five-speed stick shift, hatchback DX Honda, adorable virgin, I felt a smile in my heart, and you seemed to have a smile on your grill from headlight to headlight. I knew you'd be reliable and faithful. Your two predecessors were my '78 and '85 Hondas, and I also kept them about 11 years. I can't remember anyone driving you but me—maybe Erik, my stepson, once.

Well, as you know, I put "For Sale" signs on you, and two prospective buyers were very interested that first day, asking all kinds of questions about you. I spoke so highly of you, like a proud father: how good you've been to me; never have you given me even a minor problem; so reliable all of these 103,973 miles. And you don't use much gas: 42 plus mpg! Bravo! You're environmentally green.

I've only replaced your tires, battery, brakes, timing belt, seal beams, spark plugs, exhaust system. You are an original, only one of a kind in my heart. You never cost me a huge expense. You always passed the annual inspections with honors, as I knew you would, and I'd smile. The two prospective buyers seemed very impressed as I proudly described how you've been my Tonto and I was your Kimosabe.

I never wondered what "Kimosabe" meant listening to the Lone Ranger as a kid. I'd be transported to deep-in-the-heart-of-Texas as the white masked man and his faithful Indian companion chased, fought and caught the bad hombres. Seems odd now as I think about it, a white man and an Indian on horseback in pursuit of justice. Is it just as odd that I love you, my inanimate, non-sentient, non-spiritual faithful machine?

We've been to so many wonderful places, traveling with special people together, like when we took my sister and her husband to Tavern on the Green for their 60th anniversary and the time to the Kripalu Yoga Ashram in the Berkshires, with Ruby Cooper. I didn't want to sell you, but it's the long trips like that one to Kripalu that would cause me a lot of pain in my lower back now that I have herniated discs, stenosis and arthritis. It makes a big difference when I drive Paula's car with the cruise control. So I bought a 2007 Honda hybrid with cruise control.

Well, I'm not sure you realized what happened the second day I had the "For Sale" signs on you. This Hispanic man, a building contractor, was really interested in you. He took you for a test drive, about two to three blocks. He gunned the gas, hit the brakes hard, put on the air conditioner, etc. Yes, he was rough on you, and I wanted to protest sitting in the passenger seat: That's not the way you're used to being driven. He was very impressed, and I knew you'd passed another test.

He gave me a $500 cash deposit and wants to gift you to a woman friend—he assured me only a friend—whose husband left her with two kids and nothing else. He called her in front of me. She lives in New Jersey, and he spoke to her in Spanish before he gave me the deposit.

He says she'll have to learn how to drive a stick shift. I'm wondering: Will she be rough on your clutch? The clutch is the original! And her two young kids, screaming and climbing all over you!

What have I done to you at your age? I know you're in great shape. That's what they say about me if someone asks my age: you look good for 73! I don't think it's a compliment, but they mean it that way.

We've taken good care of each other, and we've grown old together. Perhaps I should have sold you to a more experienced driver, someone my age, who's driven a stick shift all his life. The guy who bought the car seems very nice, believing what's important in life is helping each other, especially when one is in desperate need like his friend. In these conflicting, hate-saturated, global-terrorists times, it's good to meet caring people. It's hard to let go of you, so dependable, so able and willing to be of service.

The clock is ticking. He said he'll pick you up a few days after returning from Colorado in two weeks. I've been sad, we've driven our last mile, and I won't see you around the blocks zipping by cheerfully, and I know, faithfully, now that you're going to be in Jersey.

Well, it's been 22 days since I got the deposit, and the guy hasn't returned my phone messages for the last week. I put the "For Sale" signs on again and this forty-something, soft-spoken man, who warmly said he had owned a Honda and loves them, made an offer. I accepted.

The next day someone else wanted you and offered my asking price. I said I promised you to someone yesterday who loves Hondas. After a few hours passed the first guy, the one who left the deposit then split for Colorado, showed up. He said he never got my messages because he had no cell service in the Colorado mountains; however, his woman friend did not want to learn to drive a stick shift. He apologized several times and I had no hesitation returning his full deposit because I feel good you'll be well taken care of by the guy who loves Hondas.

When I signed the title over to your new owner, I said he'd be very happy with you and to please take good care of you. He had a soft smile as he gazed at you admiringly and said, "Yes, I will."

I blew you a kiss as you drove away. You might be wondering what this love is. It's not easy to make sense of: it's like Kimosabe. As I've grown old with you, I feel closer to it. Gracious and Adios, Kimosabe, I love you. You helped me to say it.

ᰍLynn DiGiacomoᰍ

Necklacesᰍ

Was my first a ring of daisies or pop beads,
while I dreamed of being a princess?
Or was it a cross
meant to bless me in times of trouble?

The first I remember was a thin-chained
antique pendant with a sapphire chip.
It wasn't mine yet,
but I coveted its sophistication and beauty.

My own first was an intersection of
old values and new love.
A marcasite cross
given by my first boyfriend.

Then there was the Indian hippie one,
outrageously priced and courageously unorthodox.
It gave me a new identity,
jangled me into my self.

No diamonds or pearls for me;
mine would be turquoise and amber.
Bold and beautiful,
searching for statement.

Now I own the antique pendant,
but covet the girl
who dreamed of princesses and outrageous selfhood,
while I ease myself into old-aged wisdom.

꙰Lynn DiGiacomo꙰

꙰My First Love Affair

My first love affair was with Rhett Butler; no, actually it was with *Gone with the Wind*. I was in the eighth grade and ready for love. I devoured it. Certain passages made me swoon. I caressed the pages, the sentences, the very words. I waited with held breath as I turned the page. I yearned for more and more. My heart beat faster. I wanted it never to end, yet anticipated its final climax. At first I read surreptitiously, sneaking quick peeks, whetting my appetite for more. It was my mother's book, adult stuff. One day she caught me reading it when she thought I was doing homework. She didn't bat an eye. After that I read with abandon. I read it flung across my bed, draped across the hammock, curled up on the couch—in pjs, bathing suit and prim school uniform. Nothing mattered but the book. It was like withdrawal when I had to put it down. When I was not reading it, I was lusting for it. Once, my best friend Carlotta knocked on the door. I walked, book in hand, eyes glued to the page, answered the door, motioned for her to follow and continued to read. When she got mad and threatened to leave, I reached out and in true Scarlett style begged, "Oh, mercy, no." She relented and stayed, but in my heart of hearts I hoped it wouldn't be for long. I read until I was sated, and then read some more. It was the beginning of my love affair with books.

ᵍᵏLynn DiGiacomoᵏᵉ

A Slice of Life,
Not Apple Pieᵏᵉ

Images of the 50s show efficient housewives, carefully coiffed, smiling, vacuum in hand, flared dresses, turquoise-colored kitchens, in a Leave-It-to-Beaver world.

Dinner at my house was stingy. There was a scarcity of words and a scarcity of food. On my plate there was usually a piece of meat, a potato, a vegetable. They remained separate on the plate: the meat not touching the potatoes, the potatoes not touching the vegetables, and the vegetables not touching the meat. I remember margarine: white stuff with a little packet of yellow you would mix with it to make it look like butter; it never did.

My father got out of work at 4:30 and walked home from the bus stop. The slap of the screen door, wood upon wood, announced his arrival. In the crack of time before my mother arrived from work, he and my grandmother were alone together. The static between them was powerful.

"Out the way," she would say, choosing this particular time to take in the wash or straighten a curtain, and so have to nudge past my father.

Having fought a war already, he simply tried to secure the space at the head of the table.

"Humph," she'd say and return to cooking. He drank anger with his beer. I stayed away till dinnertime.

My mother in high heels and a dress would swing her long legs out of the powder blue Chevy and enter the house expecting dinner to be ready. She didn't particularly like to cook, unless it was something fancy for a party, like deviled eggs sprinkled with paprika. My grandmother, her mother, cooked, but with little enthusiasm. My mother would open the back windows to shout across the backyards, like a crow cawing:

Maaaaa - raaaaaa - lynnnnnn

and I would know it was dinnertime.

The room where we ate—the dinette—was small and cramped. The walls on either side were so close that you could barely get into the seats. There was knotty pine wallpaper halfway up the wall and a linoleum floor. The dinette set had a wood-grained Formica top. It was the kind S. Klein advertised for $59.99 a set. The edges were chipped. Sometimes I would make slight inroads on the chipped side as I sat and ate. My grandmother sat at the head of the table.

When we got a television in the early 50s, it was placed on top of the red oilcloth-covered cabinet in the kitchen. My father would adjust the rabbit ears, and it would fill the room at last with words: Hopalong-Cassidy words, Kukla-Fran-and-Ollie words, Howdy-Doody words. My brother, five years younger than I, would gape open-mouthed while my mother fed him, and I craved food I never tasted in my house.

&Lynn DiGiacomo&

Homage to a 50s Childhood&

What I remember about my home town is McLean Avenue—our Main St. I remember Shakey's malt shop, named for the owner whom I now realize must have had Parkinson's. I know it must have had another name, but we only knew it as Shakey's. There were booths in the back: one row against each wall and one in the center. I remember sitting on the stools, twirling around, ordering an egg cream or a cherry coke, and drinking it at the marble counter.

I remember the candy shop, that ten-foot-wide store where a dozen or more kids congregated on a Saturday afternoon just before the movies. We would go in there, a few pennies in hand, trying desperately to decide between the wax bottles with liquid in them or root beer barrels or Mary Janes or candy cigarettes or BB Bats or candy buttons on a paper strip. The decision was momentous, as we tried the patience of the store clerk.

I remember the Kent Theatre, under whose marquee I first fell in love. I can still see that boy, looking up at me with his lopsided grin, his blond hair falling into his eyes as he lit a cigarette. It was to that movie theater we would go every Saturday and for twenty-five cents we would see five cartoons, the "B" movie, a black-and-white newsreel, and the main feature. The usher would stride up and down the aisle, flashlight in hand, looking for disruption. The older kids were allowed to sit in the balcony, where there were rumors they "made out."

My friend Carlotta and I once a week became the stars of our own imaginations as we crept into the magic of the big screen. We danced with Ginger Rogers and swam with Esther Williams and swooned every time the leading man kissed the star, as if he were kissing us as well.

I remember Boehringer's Bakery on Sunday mornings after mass. We would all flock there to check out who was at mass, with whom, what they wore, and to share the gossip with one another. We nestled together in groups of three or four, gloves in hand, hats on head, the smell of crumb buns wafting around us, while we daydreamed of oozing jelly donuts and boys.

∽Lynn DiGiacomo∾

Swimming Together∾

It was 1963. We were twenty years old. The civil rights movement was in full force; the Beatles had just released their first album; and Betty Friedan's *The Feminine Mystique* had just begun what would be known as the Women's Movement. But these things were not on our minds as we were cruising down the New Jersey Turnpike. We held our breaths at each toll booth. The clutch chattered, and we prayed that our 1955 Ford would make it to Atlantic City—150 miles away, three hours driving time, the furthest we had ever been away from home by ourselves, the first time we had been away since we were married a year and a half ago. We had saved our money, gotten a babysitter and were on our way for the weekend. It was as if I had won the lottery and "Queen for a Day" all rolled into one.

I had seen an advertisement for a lovely old hotel with a swimming pool on the roof. I imagined cozy rooms, a charming lobby and romantic ambiance. I pictured us swimming in the pool under the stars and a full moon, music playing softly in the background. We checked in and were in our room. There was nothing lovely or romantic about it—only old, as in seedy, as in worn-flat chenille bedspread with holes in it. I sat on the bed and cried. This was shabby without the chic.

"Ernie, I can't do this! Please," I begged, "can we find another place?" Finally, my tears prevailed and we checked out and found a small motel up the block—not romantic, but not seedy either. It had tarnished my dream for the weekend, but I quickly sought to repolish it.

So it was on to the boardwalk and the beach. We had both vacationed here with our families, but we were giddy walking the boardwalk by ourselves. Ernie won a huge shaggy dog for me by hitting targets with a ball. We had a charcoal drawing done, an outrageous extravagance for us.

When we went to the beach, I attacked the waves as I usually did, fearlessly. I loved to ride them in, but usually had my lifeguard father nearby to rescue me if I got in trouble. I forgot that little detail as I got more and more courageous. With each swell I jumped, then found my footing. The rhythm of the waves and the sunlight egged me on.

"You're out too far, come back in," Ernie called to me.

"I'm okay. I'm okay."

But with the next swell I failed to touch bottom. I searched again and again for a foothold and tried to get back to shore. The sea pulled me out further and further. My heart raced as I struggled more and more. Ernie tried to help, but the more he tried the more we both were tugged out further. A lifeboat finally appeared, and I felt myself being pulled into the boat by rough strong hands. I shook from fright, cold and embarrassment as the two lifeguards rowed me back to shore, leaving Ernie to fend for himself. My eyes swept the ocean for him but couldn't find him. Back on the beach people grouped around and stared as I frantically sought Ernie's comforting embrace. Where was he? After what seemed like an eternity, there he was and we could leave this behind us. Ernie was silent as we trudged back to the hotel. I was annoyed and hurt that he wasn't more comforting after my ordeal. We closed the door to the room. Ernie collapsed on the bed and shook uncontrollably. We sat there, our arms around each other, and I realized what a marriage really is: this hadn't been my ordeal, but ours.

ᔍDiana Lindleyᔍ

The Two-Pronged Plugᔍ

My old black, boxy, ugly heater I found in the basement over ten years ago is broken. I pulled the plug out of the socket and half of the plug stayed in. For hours I feared pulling this thin piece of metal out—first it wouldn't come out, and I kept having images of being electrocuted. After I finally got it out, I tossed around the idea of buying a pretty, new, clean heater or calling my neighbor Mike to help me put a new plug on the old one. He lived through The Depression and has impressed on me how important it is to salvage things. "How could that have happened? Did you pull it out by the wire or the plug? How could a piece of it be left in the socket?" He's not criticizing, just trying to make sense of it; I'm wondering why these weird things happen but accept that they do.

I've been worrying about Mike, putting on a good front after his wife's death about a month ago. Is his joking a relief from the pressures of taking care of her in the last miserable and painful days? When he tells me he doesn't miss her after a marriage of 64 years is he being defensive? These are the kinds of things I like to dwell on, not electric plugs. I'm feeling unable to reach him these days and miss the closeness we had when our main concern was taking care of her.

He tells me which tools to bring down to his house. I have a beautiful tan and green canvas tool bag that I purchased when I first became a homeowner. It's filled with tools I have very little idea how to use, but I like them. I like their shapes and the way they feel in my hand. Mike is almost 86 years old and is in dialysis three times a week. He has a walker and not much feeling in his hands. His mind is sharp, and he is fascinated by how things work. I bring two small Phillips-head screwdrivers and what I think is a wire cutter down the icy hill to his house. Fortunately I am wearing rubber stabilizers with steel coils on the bottoms of my boots in the hopes of arriving in one piece. He is in the kitchen making lunch—pancakes poured from a bottle with sausages and syrup. He eats slowly; his sense of time stretches out while mine is clipped and hurried. He is still a handsome man with lovely, long white hair.

He does not like the two-pronged plug I have bought after a long consultation with the man at the hardware store. He worries that it is not safe, and perhaps I should get the outlets changed and bring them up to code, then buy a three-pronged plug. No, I don't have time for all this. It's cold in my study even with two sweaters and two pairs of socks, and I need the heater now. He wants to talk to me about this, which makes me feel it is important and something we need to meet about and not just rush into. I didn't think he could comfort me, but I'm really enjoying discussing this project and working together—telling me where to find the electrical tester and where to find his wire cutters with the red handles in his orange toolbox by the door. I love searching around and finding these things. He feeds the wires through the holes in the large round plug, and my job is to tighten the screws on either side. He holds the plug while I turn the Phillips-head screwdriver, his old, gnarled fingers with no feeling touching mine. His hands are large, and his touch is welcoming. I feel a frisson, an almost sexual feeling, and am taken aback that I could have these feelings for such an old man. His kind of love is not expressed in words. We have to align and realign the screws, and we have to do this several times. Mike has been telling me to "Wait a minute and slow down," for years and I still want to finish quickly. He does everything so methodically and carefully and sometimes painfully slowly with great care, which fills me with a sense of safety.

Before I leave he makes me promise that I will always turn off the heater before leaving the study, and that I will always unplug it by grasping the metal part so the wire won't get pulled off. "Promise me that in the spring you will get Tim, our local handyman and friend, to change those outlets for you." I agree.

I worry that Mike might be lonely and invite him to my house for dinner, but he doesn't want to come. It's too hard for him to get up here and negotiate my icy front yard. He wants to give me an extra spaghetti and meatball dinner from Meals on Wheels and I say no. We are very honest with each other. "She is in the hospital and she is not coming home" he told me three times, making sure that I heard and understood. I knew she was fading and dying before he did, but waited until he knew it himself. He forgets to feed the cat, a gray tabby who has lived there for fifteen years. When he is in dialysis, I go down and change her water and feed her. She is deaf and doesn't always hear me come in. He is not a cruel man, but he is not a caretaker.

"It takes you three minutes to do something that takes me about half an hour" he will say when he tells me to open something with a scissors or put something in the kitchen. This feels like high praise to me. Later, as I walk the dog, I force myself to notice the sky and the trees, take deep breaths, and try to let her sniff all those fascinating smells without dragging her back towards home.

♀Diana Lindley♀

♀Eddie's Mink

I watch ashes swirling in the ocean off the Montauk Point Lighthouse. Jim's ashes have just been scattered by his daughter and friends off the bow of the fishing boat, the *Eddie's Mink*. He captained the boat for many years, taking the owners out to deep canyons where the yellow fin tuna, so prized by the Japanese, swim. Eddie and his wife continued to pay him well into his 90s even though by then he mostly spent his time sleeping onboard.

His daughter, Paula, is wearing a man's soft gray shirt, which is much too large for her slight frame. It had rained in the morning, and the air is damp and the water that kind of iron gray that reminds me of battleships and submarines. The shirt is her father's. She made it for him and embroidered a duck on the upper right-hand pocket. He loved to hunt with his various black labs. While I was always happy to get the large pieces of tuna he would share with our family, I was relieved that we were never the recipients of a duck or other creature.

Our families became friends one day on Long Island Sound when I was about eight years old. We lived in a remote blockhouse surrounded by acres of undeveloped land, and my mother had always thought of the beach near our house as hers. One day, we spotted a small sailboat moored on the beach, and she stalked over to find out who was trespassing. When she saw that it was a couple with a baby named Paula, she fell in love, and a lifelong friendship began.

Jim died several years ago in his sleep, at home with Paula, at the age of 95. She took such good care of him and fed him such nutritious food that for a while it seemed he might make it to 100 years old. Although there is sadness among the people on the boat, it is a kind of broad sorrow about the impermanence of life. Motoring out, about twelve of his family members and my younger brother, Charles, and I chat and catch up with each other. If it wasn't for the urn and a Styrofoam cross with flowers in the cabin, it could have been a happy social gathering. Charles and Paula were inseparable as young children, and she often spent summers at our home. Once, when they were accidentally left at the beach, they continued to play happily unaware, while the adults panicked. Years later, Charles, married, and Paula, divorced, remain friendly. This day to honor Jim had been planned months ago, and family members had traveled from as far away as Puerto Rico.

I sit near Paula, feeling protective and more experienced with the rituals of death. I had lost my parents over thirty years ago, as well as several close friends. Tears pour down her face as she struggles to open the box containing what remains of her father. Of course, it is fastened with one of those plastic ties that is impossible to get off, so a knife has to be found.

She tosses some of the fine, gray ashes overboard and holds out the container to others, asking if anyone would like to take some. Everyone seems frozen in place, and I remember the sickening feeling I had when I held my first ashes with the knowledge that this was my mother. I push myself forward and grab a handful, others soon follow. Someone throws a Styrofoam cross with flowers into the water. I don't think Jim would have liked this. I never knew him to go to a church, and it's not biodegradable, just more junk in an ocean already filled with garbage. Someone reads a poem much too fast, and nobody can really hear it. The boat is pitching up and down, and I'm praying I don't throw up.

The wind blows some of his ashes back onto the damp fiberglass deck. Paula leans way over, gray shirt mingling with gray water. She fills the tin with salt water, and we both wash the ashes off the deck. It seems very important that we do this, not to clean the deck, but to honor Jim in whatever form he is in. It bonds us, and I feel really close to her. On the way back, she tells me stories of beloved animals she has had to put down over the years. Then she tells me the most intimate story of all. Her parents had been divorced for a long time. When her mother was dying, her father visited her and said, "We've had our problems, but I have always loved you." I am happy for Paula, although I'm skeptical enough to wonder how true this really was. His girlfriend of many years, and quite a close friend of mine, has told me many tales of their romantic adventures, including a marriage proposal.

On the way back home, a memory of Jim comes to me. It was fall and we had decided to take a walk in the Montauk county park, down one of our favorite trails, which led to a freshwater pond. The pond was full of memories for each of us. For Jim it held memories of his many duck hunting days with his black labs. For me, I recalled swimming there as a young girl, my long dark hair spreading out behind me among the white water lilies. Jim walked slowly by then, and we decided to rest for a while. We sat on an old wooden bench watching the sky changing colors over the pond. The sun was setting and my treasured dog, Auggie, lay by our side. We shared the silence. So contented and at peace. No place to be and no place to go. No one saying we should be getting home soon.

O Pioneer!◈

As "Show Boat" continued to play to empty houses, it became apparent to us that the theater would have to close. All the advertising in the world was not going to bring people to Alaska that summer. Realizing that we would not be staying until October as we had originally planned, we decided that we had better see something of Alaska before we left. We made plans with the Californians from upstairs to fly up to the Arctic Circle. We found a very competent woman to stay with the children and flew off to explore an Inuit Indian village just north of the Arctic Circle. There were no roads leading north from Fairbanks at that time, and the countryside that we flew over was barren and colorless. The Indian village depended on tourists like us who were intent on exploring the country above the Arctic Circle.

Another tourist attraction that we wanted to see was Denali National Park. We had flown over Mount McKinley on that first night we arrived in Alaska, but we wanted to take the train ride from Fairbanks along the Chena River into the park. Meanwhile, in addition to the earthquake aftershocks that continued to plague us, it started to rain. It rained day and night for more than a week. As we had expected, the theater closed. My husband had a contract that required that he be paid through October, so while the theater management tried to figure out where they would find the money to honor our contract, we bought our train tickets to Denali and planned to be tourists for a day.

We never got to Denali. The train ride to Mount McKinley was canceled when the rainwaters washed out the railroad bridge into the park. The theater management offered to give us the green Volkswagen microbus in lieu of my husband's salary. Being the adventurers that we were and knowing that this may be our only way out of Alaska, we accepted. We quickly made plans to drive from Alaska to New York City with our five children in the microbus.

When I get to this part of this story, most people roll their eyes and look at me as if they are speaking to a crazy woman. Not so! I was young and energetic and had never seen most of the country. We had lots of free time since my husband was no longer employed. The only thing that I regret about that trip is that the children were not old enough to remember it.

We headed out of Fairbanks south to the Alcan Highway. We had made extensive preparations for this trip. We purchased two infant car beds for the twins who were now nearly three months old. These were the days before bottled water so I boiled enough water for infant formula to last for three weeks. We stored this in large red five-gallon containers. We bought a tent and sleeping bags to use on those nights that we could not find a motel room. Greg and Jon did not want to leave the tricycles behind so we tied them to the rack on the top of the bus. We said goodbye to our California friends and the rest of the theater company, and we were on our way.

The Alcan Highway was a three-thousand-mile dirt road from Delta Junction, just south of Fairbanks, Alaska, to Dawson Creek in British Columbia, Canada. It is carefully marked with mileposts and signs to indicate how far it is to the next rest stop, gas station, restaurant, motel or campground. These are mostly situated approximately fifty miles apart. The highway is patrolled by the Army Corps of Engineers, which is ready to deal with any problems that may arise. We felt perfectly safe even though we were traveling through total wilderness and saw very few cars along the way.

The rain continued for the next two days. As we traveled south, the Alaskan Coastal Mountains were a constant view several miles in the distance on our right. We could actually see streams of water forming on the sides of the mountain, like silver ribbons flowing toward the highway.

᠙Denise Gray Meehan᠙

᠙Spring Cleaning

My year-old grandson's favorite toy is a toddler-size vacuum cleaner, and that gets me a little nervous. I try to sterilize the house before he and his father, Mr. Clean, come to visit, but I will never meet their standards. If cleanliness is next to godliness, I will be spending a lot of time vacuuming in purgatory.

I used to wonder what the big deal was about spring cleaning. I thought putting screens up and opening windows was sufficient. My mother, a talented decorator, was not a good role model for housekeeping. On Saturday mornings my father, whose dresser drawers were alphabetically arranged, would blast a ceremonial march on the stereo. Yelling "rise and shine" before breakfast, he would assign and then supervise cleaning chores. I know this was a mother-driven idea. Since he was usually playing golf, which my mother always resented, this probably only happened once or twice. But it is imprinted in my memory.

After the fourth of five daughters was born, Mrs. Isabelle Halpin started arriving at our house on Thursday mornings. We lived in Great Neck; she lived in Little Neck. She had five sons; we became her five girls. Halp and Mom began their mornings with coffee and cigarettes at the glass table in the blue-and-white onion-print-wallpapered breakfast nook. Tall and angular, Halpin would grind the life out of her lipstick-smeared Parliament butt and then get to work.

When we moved to a town further east, she followed. When my parents went on vacations, she'd stay with us. We used to joke that our mother needed a little "halp." My sister

Suzan and I would stay up late with her watching Perry Mason and dragging on our mother's cigarettes while Halp spoke conspiratorially to us about our boyfriends. If a younger sister wanted to play hooky, all she had to do was to promise to massage Halp's head. Every year there was a new aliment that prevented her from bending, kneeling, lifting and/or pushing. A soap opera fan, she spent hours ironing in the basement watching "General Hospital," "As the World Turns" and "All My Children." Everything in our house was starched.

My sister Jennifer is living proof that housekeeping is not an inherited trait because she used to stay home from school to clean on Fridays. She couldn't stand it if certain things like the top of the refrigerator or under the couch couldn't pass her white glove test. It was such a problem that my mother hired another cleaning woman to come the day after Halpin. Finally, after several of our weddings, Mrs. Halpin was offered a full-time job at the rectory. My mother, who after all those years was still Mrs. Gray, told her to take the job for all its benefits, that somehow we would manage without her.

Later in life I mentioned to my mother that her current cleaning lady hadn't disturbed the colony of dust bunnies living under the couch in the TV room. She said that at her age it was a blessing that vision faded along with the memory and that the house smelled good after so and so left. I wanted to say, "And you, too, can spray Pledge in the air," but my mother always saw the world through rose-colored glasses.

My former mother-in-law used to ask me what color my daughter Melissa's gently scuffed white shoes were. And at the end of holiday meals I was usually still eating pumpkin pie while the vacuum was sucking crumbs around me. In my mother's house we lay on the living room floor like beached whales after dinner — dessert came later — and the clean-up was a gradual process often involving the next day or two.

While I was working on my Master's, I took a marine studies course that basically involved field trips. Two other women and I decided to car pool. Both blondes had immaculate white cars — a Volvo station wagon with no trace of the dogs who were regular passengers and the other a white Mercedes. It was my turn to drive. I had fully intended to clean my grey VW Cabriolet convertible, but it had rained heavily the night before. I removed the bulk of coffee cups, papers and other signs that suggested I might be living in my car, but I did not vacuum. After we met at our spot, one of my new friends wedged into the rear corner of my car and asked to have the shotgun seat moved forward to give her a little more leg room, and what had been a bagel with vegetable cream cheese rolled to her feet. True friendships survive these types of imperfections.

The irony is that another friend and I had a cleaning business for two summers. I was just looking for some extra cash in my pocket. Suddenly I had twelve college girls working for me, and we were sweeping in the money. Our company was called Country Clean. Our logo was an outline of a red house, the type you see on quilts, and we all wore white shirts and red Bermuda shorts. My partner was the right hand; I was the left. She saw the big picture, and I would focus on the area around the kitchen sink drain, deftly buffing it with a toothbrush. I loved having my own business, but I didn't love cleaning toilets.

So, I am not a slob, but my mirrors-and-smoke approach to housekeeping is similar to my early entertaining strategy: ply your guests with copious cocktails, so by the time dinner is served they are just glad to eat. I'm a much better cook these days, but I still believe in low lights and lots of candles. In the final moments, I stash and hide offending piles and objects under couches and in drawers. The dryer also comes in handy. I am getting smart in my old age. Now I try to schedule parties the day after my cleaning lady comes. I am my mother's daughter.

꒰Denise Gray Meehan꒱

November꒱

Sweet-potato gold leaves still cling sunlit to the trees. Russet red, parched persimmon and caramelized chestnut hues make the eye hungry for more. This has been the longest lasting autumnal display I can remember. But the leaves are letting go now, and soon their skeletal branches will outline the graying sky as winter bullies its way in. And death seems to be everywhere.

My father died in 1996. Occasionally I don't remember the date, but I will never forget the day we inhaled his last exhale on that November morning. So I associate death with the eleventh month. Not mid-month yet and I have heard of two deaths and three imminent ones. Before he died Vince Cannuscio wrote to our local newspaper in the viewpoint column and entitled it a "Love Letter." He began by stating that his daughter always ended their conversations with "I love you." He'd reply that she didn't need to say it. But now that the number of times he will hear those words are limited, he realized that he was wrong. He said "thank you" in a very personal and public way to the town that embraced him as supervisor, caring citizen, good friend and neighbor.

I think of "D" words. In addition to the words that begin with the negative "de" and "dis" prefixes, "d" words are death, devil, down, dirty, dour, dank, and dull. Unlike the "s" words that are scintillating, sexy, slippery, silky, and sleek.

November comes from Latin *novem*, which means "nine" for the ninth month of the early Roman calendar. July and August were added later to honor Julius and Augustus Caesar. It's interesting that November begins with the first three letters of the Latin root *novus,* meaning new. But November isn't the ninth month or the beginning of a new season.

Maybe this Thanksgiving, besides the traditional blessings, we should think of novel things for which to be thankful. Perhaps we could begin with a new president and the renewal of hope. Death to the days when "all men are created equal" were hollow words.

❧Gail Zappone❧

Fake It Till You Make It❧

Faking it doesn't normally fit my personality or values when it comes to how I communicate with people. Yet, when I look back on my life and how I've motivated myself to do things that might have been a little out of reach, I see that it is a strategy that I have used many times. And I'd like to think that most times it has worked for me.

I can remember at the age of 19, I finished business school and started to take interviews for secretarial positions in New York City. Going into the city to look for a job seemed like a drag. Entering employment offices with interviewers whose first words might be, "Can you type?" even before they said "Hello," following up ads in the classifieds for entry-level clerk/typist positions that stated, "Must have high energy, be willing to work overtime, have excellent references, type 90 words a minute with dictation 120 wpm, be willing to take a speed and spelling test," sent me into a sea of intimidation that would either start a migraine or coughing spell.

Rejection seemed inevitable, as a typing test would begin and my fingers would get caught between the keys or a typo would occur. I would slow down to improve and all of a sudden the test would be over and I would have five more errors than I was supposed to have—an immediate failure. Discouragement would set in. Negative thoughts would flow. I'm never going to find anything. Look at me. I'm shy. I don't know how to "sell myself," I'm nervous, I speak too slowly. I'm a mess. Where's my confidence. If I can't even convince myself, how am I ever going to convince anyone else?

After my first week of "pounding the pavement," I started to feel sorry for myself. I almost started to feel like the guy in the song singing "Buddy can you spare a dime." Spending more and more time in Horn & Hardart's (sipping coffee—looking over newspaper ads for jobs I was unqualified for), I began to feel worse.

One day I was so low, I decided to play hooky. I went over to Central Park, sat on a bench and let the sun just shine down on my face and warm me up. It was spring and everyone was out there. I started to look at all the people, young and old, walking along. It was like a movie. No, no, it was like a play. Like Shakespeare said hundreds of years ago, "All the world's a stage"…and we're the actors, or something like that. My observations of people (the actors) started to be more concentrated. I began evaluating who looked successful, who looked happy, who looked down and out, and who looked like they had a chip on their shoulder or the weight of the world.

Then I focused in on young people my age. One woman, not much older than me, came walking toward me with a positive attitude. You could see that she knew where she was going. She had self-confidence. She was in an attractive business suit and was well groomed. Her heels clicked with purpose. A slight smile of self-awareness seemed to cross her lips. People turned to look. She seemed to make an impact and knew it.

I couldn't sit still then. Whatever it was, whatever she had, I knew just sitting there wasn't going to make it happen for me. So I got up, inspired by this girl, and started walking. My mind became alert to everything around me, and I was energized for the first time in a week. I was on a quest. I could do it. I had something to offer. I had a diploma, a business school certificate, references, some experience.

I marched down the street to the first department store I passed, walked in and went straight to the handbag department. I said to the saleslady, "Do you carry briefcases for women?" She pointed me toward a selection of the type of bags I had been noticing on the street. I said, "I'll take that shiny, black leather one with the gold buckle. She said, "Do you want me to wrap it up for you?" I said, "No, that's okay, I'll carry it." I emptied my backpack. My lunch, *War and Peace* and a few other items dropped out. I gave her the old, beat-up bag. She said, "What do you want me to do with this?" I said, "Oh, you can just throw it out." I thanked her and waltzed out of the store swinging my new briefcase. I felt like Gene Kelly in *Singin' in the Rain*!

≈Gail Zappone≈

ᕦResolution

There they are again. As I knock over my old Frye boots once again in my closet, strewn with shoes, slippers, sneakers, heels and boots, I sigh and ask the question, "When are you finally going to wear those boots, for Chrissakes!" You carted them from New York City to Westchester to the rented house to the cottage in K'town (Katonah), and after all the soul-searching and wading through tons of black garbage bags going to the Salvation Army, there were the boots, ready to make it out to Southampton. "Maybe in my retirement," I said, "I'll get back to my roots, wear my old long skirts, and those boots will go great with them."

We had put so much into storage when we moved out to the Island. Our seaside home was not much bigger than a three-bedroom apartment. But the boots got a VIP seat in the closet two years ago and have not moved since, except to topple over and say "Hello, excuse me…is there a plan for me or is the show over, because you can tell me. It won't hurt my feelings. I will survive—I'm sure, if you send me to Good Will, I can be someone else's salvation. Please either commit or I'm outta here!"

I did break down and put boot trees in them and polish and weatherize them, until they had a nice shine and looked pretty good in a nice soft light rust color a few months ago, but still, not even a rehearsal. I close the door in shame. I say to myself, "This Fall, I WILL wear the boots. They will see the light of day again."

≈Gail Zappone≈

Wanderlust≈

Browsing through a gift catalog, I spotted a picture of a bracelet engraved with the quote, "All those who wander are not lost." I stopped and thought, "That's it! That's me! I have those words engraved on my heart—and spirit." Even reading the words caused my heart to leap. As long as I can remember (or as my mother would say, "...as soon as she could walk!"), I was off and down the road.

Exploring the world in my toddler state meant checking out all the birds and flowers in my backyard. Mom would say, looking out the kitchen window above, "Now, for heaven's sake, don't go anywhere." But as soon as I had checked out everything in the yard I would squeeze through the hedge, and I was off. Down the block into the woods where the trees, larger than life, seemed to be calling me. They shaded the sky from my view. The rays of sunshine streaming down added a bit of magic to my adventure. I could stay there for hours wandering through weeds and wildflowers, listening to the echo of the birds and the distant sounds of the outside world.

This was heaven to me, and I would create little games and plays all by myself. Once I finished creating something—a nest to play in or a skit to act out, as I got older—I would bring back the neighborhood kids to show them the freedom of this enchanted world. This woodland became a sacred place for all of us, a place where we could go. And, better than a clubhouse, it was outside and yet somewhat protected. When a mom or dad couldn't find any of us, they would go to the edge of the woods where there was a diagonal path that had an imaginary chain. There they would holler our names, never dreaming of entering our world. When we heard them and one of our gang had to leave, immediate sympathy went round the whole group, as if we had been invaded. I loved to climb trees, and our games of tag were very elaborate. They would generally be connected to a fairy tale or movie that we had seen in the local movie theater. We would be acting it out and, if it required hiding or getting away, up a tree I would go. Actually, I had the reputation of being the best climber on the block.

One day when we were acting out one of these adventures, I was "IT" and chasing a tough kid from a different block. Pinky was a year or so younger then me. Although I didn't know him well, he seemed like a rough, mean guy. He didn't know what a good climber I was as he jumped up in a tree to get away from me. I climbed right after him, saying to myself, "Oh yeah. Let's see how far you go." Pinky went to extremes. I would almost catch him, and he would slip away. I guess he was a better climber than I had realized. But I was determined. He lost sight of me on a branch, and all of a sudden there he was, way out at the end of the same branch I was on. I screamed out in a panic, "Pinky, no!!" But it was too late. As the branch cracked, instinctively he jumped to another branch. I, on the other hand, froze. I felt myself free fall like a piece of fruit, whoosh, straight down.

I landed twenty feet down on the hard, damp earth below, right on my tailbone. The wind was knocked out of me, and I couldn't breathe. I fell over to the side to get some relief and to try to help fresh air come back into my lungs. It seemed like an eternity. Meanwhile, I was encircled by the kids. They stood there, frozen, watching me try to gasp for air. I fought to breathe harder than I can ever remember. Pain had finally reached my mind, but I knew, instinctively, that I had to put it aside. My brain was kicking into automatic and doing everything it could do to help fix me—like a mechanic bent over a car, working on the motor.

Suddenly a loud, weird noise came out of my mouth and nose at the same time. If we had been fooling around, everyone would have been laughing and rolling on the ground by now. But the sound created a sense of fear in all of us. It was a barometer of how serious this might be. I was afraid to move, so I just sat there resting one elbow on the ground for leverage and continued to try to breathe. Little by little, my breath started to come more regularly. By now I was more aware of my surroundings and started to feel a little embarrassed as I sat in the middle of this circle with everyone staring at me. So I started to move, slowly. As I did, the base of my spine cried out in sharp pain. I decided to take it much slower. One of the kids gave me a hand, then another and another, until everyone was helping me up. I limped along slowly. Somehow, I don't remember actually getting home or what my mother thought when she saw me or anything else, because I was so glad that I could breathe. I could walk. My days of wandering would not be over.

꧁Gail Zappone꧂

꧁Running Out of Time

The day before I died I had a lot of things to get done. But I couldn't find the list. "Now wait a minute," I said, "it was right here." I sighed. "Retrace your steps," my mother used to say. "What were you just doing?" So I took a deep breath and concentrated. "Now where was I when I wrote the list? Think back. Okay. I know I was running out of time, and there were thousands of things to get done. I was getting discouraged as I was writing things down." And then I said to myself, "Oh! You'll never get THAT done! You don't have enough time. Don't panic, just write. Write whatever comes into your mind. You can cross out later." So I started to write: "Take out the garbage, make the bed, brush your teeth, take a shower."

"Hey, wait a minute," I thought disgustedly. "This is not an ordinary day. This is your LAST day. What are you going to do to make an impact? You need to go out in style. You could throw a party! Not enough time! You could take a short trip into the city—see a play, take in a museum. Not enough time! I know. You could plan your LAST meal. Naah! Reminds me too much of prison."

"That's it!" I threw the list away. It was not helping. The only thing on the list that vaguely sounded good was "Take a shower." So I took a nice, hot shower. I started humming, "Singin' in the Rain," one of my favorite mood songs. Pretty soon I was belting it out. Then I even started dancing around the room. I was on a roll.

This can't be my last day! I feel too good. I have so much to do. There's the election. Every vote counts! I can't let them down. I must be there. What about the environment? Now there's a problem that's not going to be solved overnight. And my family—my family—so much loving and sharing to still give. Besides, no will—I didn't write a will. My kids will say, "No will—what was she thinking!" "Doesn't she know—everybody leaves a will?" My husband and I just never got around to it.

They must be wrong. I'm not finished. I'll go another time. No one will notice. People are always late.

❧The Cloisters

I have photographs of my castle, which is high on a hilltop in a wooded area of Fort Tryon Park overlooking Dyckman Street. It is called The Cloisters, a museum that displays the medieval collection of the Metropolitan Museum of Art from European monasteries and secular castles and estates.

We moved from East 169th Street, in the Bronx, to the Inwood section of Manhattan in 1945. I was one and a half years old. My mother said she would walk with my older sister and me up the pathway from Dyckman Street or through the A train subway tunnel at 190th Street and take the elevator that opened onto Fort Washington Avenue at the entrance to The Cloisters. I do not remember. The first walk through The Cloisters that I can remember was when I was eight years old and I was terrified. My mother was wheeling my baby sister, a toddler, in her stroller. I was holding on to one side, my older sister on the other. We were about to enter the chapel that displayed the tombs. My mother saw I was upset and explained that the tombs were very old and no longer held dead people.

After that walk, The Cloisters became my castle, a magical place where I imagined ladies of the court sitting before the huge fireplace working on their embroidery. The weavers sitting at their looms making The Unicorn Tapestries. The monks chanting in the garden. People walking on a staircase that now does not go through to another floor.

Mother took us to The Cloisters many times. Once, when we walked up the steps, she showed us the lamppost where during World War II a German spy had hidden his stolen documents. When we toured The Cloisters she read the descriptions that were on the wall next to a tapestry or art object. "What's that? What's that?" we said, as we walked through the various rooms. She pointed out the plants in the herb garden and told us how they were once used for medicine. She showed us the "Chalice of Antioch," which was discovered in 1910 and at the time was thought to be "The Holy Grail." Best of all were The Unicorn Tapestries, because I liked horses. Unicorns were horses with horns, Mother explained; unicorns did not exist, but centuries ago people did think they were real.

When I was thirteen or fourteen, I was allowed to go through the park without an adult. I would go with my sisters and friends. In those days there was no admission charge, and we would go often. My best friend showed me another way to get to the top of the hill. We climbed the "Indian steps," a steep, narrow stone-step trail through the woods, past the campsites of the homeless people. (The Indians didn't make the steps, and my mother never knew about them.) We sat on the wall in the herb garden and did our homework or read a book. There were very few security guards; we were never asked to move. We walked around and watched other people's reactions as they viewed the art. We thought it was odd that some people touched or rubbed the statues of the numerous saints. Some quietly said a prayer before a statue, just as if the statue was still in a church or cathedral.

During the years I was in nursing school, I did not get up to The Cloisters very often. When I graduated and was working and attending college, I was able to spend more time at The Cloisters with my friends. We once saw a bridal party being photographed, and I told my friends "This is where I want to be married, overlooking the Hudson River."

Ten years later, in January 1973, at The Cloisters, a medical student and I were sitting on the low stone wall at the Chapter House. He had recently completed his rotation at the hospital where I worked. We had taken care of a seriously ill patient together. As we talked, he told me that it was at that patient's bedside that he had fallen in love with me. He asked me to marry him. He wanted me to move to Alabama with him and open a rural practice. I said "No!" It was only our first date. (It was also our last.) As we got up to leave, a young boy about six years old was hiding behind the wall, listening.

In the 1980s I moved to Yonkers with my family and did not go to The Cloisters as often. I had purchased several books at the museum gift shop and often read about the symbolism represented in The Unicorn Tapestries.

My last trip to The Cloisters was five years ago with friends. The courtyard was packed with tour buses. The admission charge was twelve dollars, and we rented audio tours. The rooms were now temperature and humidity controlled, and more artifacts were in glass cases. Security guards scrutinized everyone's movements and rushed to close the door when a room was entered. No one was allowed to sit on the walls in the gardens, and everyone was told, "Please don't touch the statues." My castle of long ago had become a modern, crowded and noisy museum.

The way I will remember The Cloisters is not the way it is now, but as it was when I was eight years old, a place that seemed far away from the hot city streets. A world of make-believe, where "there was a time when people believed that unicorns existed." The unicorns to me as a child were very real. I did believe the legend. Unicorns did once live in the woods, just like they had been woven into the tapestries. They were off playing and forgot to get on the Ark.

๛Eva Lucatuorto ๛

Spaghetti on Paper Plates๛

When I was a child and my paternal grandfather was still living, the family picnic was always on a Sunday. My father worked every Saturday; therefore family picnics had to be scheduled for Sunday so the entire family could attend. This was like all the Sunday dinners at my grandfather's house in Astoria, Queens: no excuses, except for serious illness.

The preparation for a picnic or attendance at our Italian hometown feast always took multiple phone calls. Who was going to the ice house to pick up the blocks of ice, who was going to the "Hammer" beverage factory in the Bronx, who was going to the pie bakery in Astoria, Queens, to pick up the pies, who would order and pick up the special Italian, hometown lamb sausage at the butcher shop in "Little Italy" in the Bronx? However, buying the pastries was always assigned to my oldest uncle; the Italian bakery was on the ground floor of the apartment building where he lived.

We went to many different parks for our picnics. Picking out a new picnic site was not easy. There were criteria that had to be met. The picnic grounds had to be close to the parking lot, there had to be running water and bathrooms (although some were quite primitive) and there had to be shade trees.

This particular Sunday one of my uncles was delegated to get to the picnic ground at dawn and move as many as ten tables into a row and set up the grills to cook breakfast. This meant my parents did not have to be the first family there, and my sisters and I could sleep later. When my parents woke us, my older sister and I left the apartment in our pajamas and climbed into my parents' 1939 Chevy. My younger sister was a baby; she was carried down to the car and placed in the portable baby carriage on the seat between my older sister and me. The carriage was balanced on the seat and the bump in the middle of the floor (the undercarriage with the wheels was placed in the trunk). I always sat behind the passenger seat where my father sat. My father never had a driver's license, so my mother did all the driving.

The car trunk of a 1939 Chevy was very small; the picnic supplies that did not fit in the trunk were under our feet in the back and beside my father's legs in the front.

My father's cousin lived down the street with his wife and with his son who was nineteen months older than me and the same age as my older sister. Their car was double-parked, and they were waiting to follow our car. Sometimes, if we did not know the area where the picnic was being held, we would drive over to the Bronx, and my father's oldest brother would lead us in his car. My mother could have followed the directions, but this is the way it had to be done. Sometimes we had a line of five or six cars, and each car had to have a white or red scarf or rag tied onto the antenna. All the cars had to have the headlights on. If someone lagged behind or got separated, all the other cars had to pull over and wait. I always thought we looked like a funeral procession, but without hearse and flower cars.

Somewhere along the ride to the picnic grounds, my older sister and I changed into our clothes. When we arrived at the picnic grounds, we jumped out of the car and helped carry everything over to a table.

Under a tree in the big, round, galvanized washtubs, with blocks of ice surrounded by ice chips, were bottles of milk and soda. The cases of seltzer and ice picks were on the ground. A large case of egg cartons was on the table, along with stacks of paper plates and paper cups.

Our breakfast of bacon and eggs was cooking on the charcoal grills. There were also coffeepots and saucepans of water to heat up the baby bottles. These pots stayed on one of the grills all day into the night.

The grills were all identical, except for the legs, which were painted different colors for identification by the owners. Each one was a large bakery pan about thirty inches in length, about twenty-four inches in width and three to four inches deep. Holes were drilled in the bottom for ventilation, and the legs were removable as they were attached at the sides of the four corners of the pan with two nuts and wing bolts. There were no braces for the legs, which were about a yard in length and had to be pushed into the ground to stabilize them. The skewers were aluminum and about 35 inches by ½ inch and were filed to sharp points at one end. My father owned eight skewers, and the pointed ends hung off the back of the grill pan. All the children were cautioned to stay away from the backs of the grills.

One uncle always had rolls of white paper that he rolled down one side of each table and back up on the other side. My mother then spread out a brightly colored oilcloth tablecloth and put out her silverware.

As soon as everyone had breakfast, the big pots of water for spaghetti would go on the grill. It took a long time for the water to boil. All the cousins would play catch or other games. My older sister and I always had our pink rubber Spaulding balls with our names written on them in ink. This always saved a lot of fighting throughout the day. Some of my uncles and cousins would pitch horseshoes. Other aunts and uncles would play cards or sit around and talk.

For lunch the men grilled chicken and sausage. Each thin sausage link had to be coiled inward from each end and then skewered through the middle of the coils. It was always done this way. Even if we fried it at home in a pan for dinner, it had to be coiled this way. The chicken was marinated with oil and vinegar as it cooked, using a lettuce leaf instead of a brush. The flames that shot up were calmed with a sprinkling of salt. Someone would make the meat sauce, which had pork, hot sausage, meatballs, stuffed skin and my favorite, braciole.

Everyone was called to the table, and mounds of spaghetti topped with the rich homemade meat sauce was served on paper plates, along with the grilled lamb sausage and salad. Italian bread was in the middle of the table; the long loaves were torn apart, and the round loaves were cut with a large knife by one of the men holding the large loaf against his stomach. There was plenty of soda for the kids, American coffee and red wine with seltzer for the adults. For dessert there was fresh fruit, with thick wedges of cheese, coconut custard pies and the Italian pastries, which were filled or smothered with cheese custard or whipped cream. The adults also had hot, thick, black Italian coffee, with a few drops of anisette. Dinner was a repeat of lunch, although there seemed to be non-stop eating all day long.

At sunset my mother and aunts would clear the tables and wash off the tablecloths that had been stained with red-colored oil that had seeped through the paper plates. The cars were packed up, the sleeping babies were carried to the cars, and we all left the parking lot in a parade of red and white car lights

꙰Eva Lucatuorto ꙰

Tales of Star, My Labrador Retriever꙰

Part I: The Thief

I wanted a dog
My sister helped me choose
The puppy out of the litter
That carried off her handbag
That was sitting on the floor
And when I brought him home
Stole my father's shoes

He chose to take anything unguarded
A tomato paste lid
On top of his tongue
A razor blade beneath his paw
And when I found them
There was never a drop of blood

Down the long dark hallway
He carried a raw egg in his mouth
To his bathroom hiding place
When I asked him to drop it in my hand
Held under his mouth
He chose to crack it
And let the white and gold ooze over my palm

He sat with each treasure between the toilet and the wall
He must have been amazed when he grew and no longer fit
Then he found the clawfoot tub
And claimed it once and for all as his

He stole a half-eaten turkey
From my buffet table
Carried it past me as my guests said goodbye
He had turkey dinners for a week
While I ate canned tuna fish

Best of all
I'm sure he always thought
Were the treasures from my handbag
That was sitting on the floor
For sixteen years he never trained me
To keep it off the floor

Part II: The Children

I hear the hysterical screams.
I run down the long, dark hallway of our Manhattan
apartment.
My older sister stands frozen on the threshold of the
living room.
Grasping the French door, she continues to scream.
Between screams she yells
"My child is being poisoned."
I look into the living room
My toddler niece, dressed in her immaculately clean pink
dress, is on the floor
She is chewing one end of Star's gel bone.
Star is on the other
I pick her up.
Crying, she reaches her small arms downward toward Star.

ও   ও

Home from work. I walk down the long, dark hallway.
At the French door of the living room,
I hear my mother quietly say,
"Don't wake them."
Star is on his side sleeping on the faded Oriental rug
On his chest is my sleeping toddler nephew's head.
His tiny fingers clasp his half-empty bottle against his plaid
flannel shirt.
I sit silently on the green sofa next to my mother.
My nephew wakes.
I pick him up.
He gives me a sleepy smile, and then giggles.

❧Hands On

Two or three mornings a week I climb into my blue Jeep and venture down Hill Street to Radu's fancy gym, where over the next ninety minutes or so, I methodically tear down my hands. The principal instrument of destruction is the bench press, an elementary exercise for developing the chest but also the arms and shoulders. The bench press, a fixture in every serious lifter's routine, also serves as a yardstick for the core discipline of pumping iron, much as a smooth Hollandaise sauce might be our measure of a classical cook or a crisp, clean drive our gauge of a golfer. The bench press is by no means the only exercise I do, but it is the one I always do first and the one that has me hooked.

As you might guess, you execute a bench press by lying face up on a bench, your feet planted firmly on the floor, under a steel bar supported by a rack. The bar, which itself weighs forty-five pounds, has iron doughnut-like discs slipped on each end, in various combinations of sizes. The usual gym complement starts with discs as light as two-and-one-half pounds and goes up to forty-five pounds (twenty kilos in the metric system). The exercise consists of spreading your arms wide, grasping and then lifting the bar-plus-doughnuts off the rack, and, thus burdened, extending your arms toward the ceiling. Normally you do one or more sets of ten repetitions each. Ideally you add weights and sets to the point where you can lift the tenth repetition but barely and not a repetition more.

I begin with sets of one hundred pounds and work up in jumps until I'm straining to lift one-eighty-five a mere two or three times. Bench pressing is very much a progressive endeavor, appealing to people with minds like The Little Engine That Could. *I think I can, I think I can, I think I can.* The essence of becoming hooked is the challenge of hoisting five more pounds this week than I could last. Actually no one advances at that pace. Progression is much slower, much more difficult. But as with learning a foreign language, the frustration of getting nowhere fast is rewarded periodically with an immensely gratifying advance.

Some three years ago, in an initial outing, I managed to press eighty pounds (and *that* left my chest and shoulders sore for a week). Last April on my birthday, I lifted two hundred and five (at least twice), finally attaining a grail of bench-pressing my weight. I had selected that goal shrewdly, figuring it opened *two* paths to success: lift more or weigh less. My weight did drop back a few pounds from my peak, but over the entire tenure of pumping iron, I've gained about twenty pounds, net. My jacket size jumped from a 42 to a 46, so apparently not all that gain came at my waist. If you take a close look at my arms, you can detect decent muscle tone. And at sixty-eight going on sixty-nine, I am far, far stronger than I've ever been in my life. The satisfaction from that runs a lot deeper than just making it easier to manhandle bags of groceries from the car. And I did *earn* it—hundreds of gym sessions, hundreds of tons.

I have paid the price in my hands. As you lift, your palms, especially the cradle between thumb and forefinger, become the bearing points. All that massive iron crushes down on them, as much as a hundred pounds on each hand. Though the fundamental dynamic of weight-lifting requires tearing down muscle fiber so it can grow back stronger, it's clear I have asked too much of my fingers and thumbs. No muscle has torn or broken down—yet. My hands are not swollen, but my fingers are numb. My thumbs are slow to flex. I have lost an appreciable amount of my small-motor skills.

I can no longer master a pen. No one would have given me an award for penmanship, but I did come of age in the day when a clear, flowing script was prized. Both in school and later at work, I would take copious notes. I never duplicated the wonderfully clear script the third grade teacher posted on parents' night, but my handwriting could be read by anyone. Now my pen wanders all over the road, like a drunk driver who eluded the late-night road check. The fingers gripping the pen can't reverse field in time to close a loop or make the small wiggles that go into a tidy, neat hand. The pen point veers 'way too far in rounding the curve; I pull it back and overcorrect, swinging as far off the track the other way.

I no longer write my own name. With deliberation I get through the opening *Andr* well enough but the *ews* collapses into a mere squiggle. When it comes to signing credit card chits — especially those electronic versions — I scarcely bother. I press the electronic pen to the surface and give my arm a good shake.

My fingertips have lost sensitivity. Buttoning a shirt, once done nimbly, absent-mindedly, while focusing on other things, takes concentration, and even a certain amount of groping, for my fingers to locate and align the buttonhole. I think of Bob Dole and his withered right arm, the legacy of a terrible war wound. Supposedly he struggles for half an hour to button his shirt. I don't know how he stands the frustration of coming just this close to nudging a button into the right slot, only to miss and have to begin all over again.

Of all the things we take for granted, our hands must be among the most precious. I recall forty years ago, when President Kennedy's assassination was still a raw wound, his widow Jackie said of his brother Robert: "I'd put my hand in the flame for that man." You knew right away what incredible solace he must have offered to her. And to the extreme of cruelty, was anything worse than the Sudanese rebels who maliciously maimed instead of killed (though they did that, too)? They hacked off captives' hands above the wrist, condemning their surviving victims to a life of infant-like dependence on others for the simplest of tasks. I once saw a film clip of one despairing fellow being spoon-fed supper by his son, a lad of ten. My modest diminution is nowhere close to either extreme. Those chance memories serve only to remind me what's at stake. I would go immediately to an orthopedist, except that he would tell me to stop lifting weights.

҆Fred Andrews҆

҆One Man's Life

In my sunset years I opted to become a fireman, the oldest rookie in the known history of the Southampton (Volunteer) Fire Department, protecting greater Southampton since 1881. Last year I whipped through the classroom stuff and survived the hands-on boot camp at the Fire Academy at Yaphank, up island. A crisp certificate carrying the signature of Governor Pataki attests to my qualifications to enter a burning structure—prudently on hands and knees and burdened, like my brothers and occasional sisters, with sixty-two pounds of gear: the thick tan turnout coat and pants; those clumsy rough leather gloves; the helmet, face mask and air tank, right down to the heavy rubber boots with steel inserts in the soles.

But that's not my job. With due allowance for aging knees and diminishing flexibility, I am fire police. Mainly we control traffic at a fire or accident scene. Though I take the obligation most seriously (not counting meetings and drills, I answered 141 calls last year, albeit the vast majority trivial), I'm accustomed to describing the experience as something of a lark, The Marx Brothers Meet Towering Inferno. By my bemused telling, I am an aging Don Quixote. Jocular or not, I do understand that the fire service holds life or death in its hands. A sobering thought.

It is Thursday, January 26, 2007, a frigid midwinter evening. I am standing in the intersection of Hillcrest Avenue and North Sea Road in Southampton Village. Half a block up Hillcrest two dozen or so firefighters are trying to knock down a blazing fire in a modest house on the north side of the street, just down from the church. An eighty-one-year-old man fell asleep with a lit cigarette in his hand.

That half block of Hillcrest is clogged with two fire engines and two hook and ladder trucks; the three fire chiefs' SUVs; a couple of police cars, and the Southampton Volunteer Ambulance. Lines of five-inch hose snake up the hill from the hydrant down at my corner. Three more trucks are parked along North Sea Road, having dispatched their crews to the scene. From this distance I can see a couple of "truckies"—the hook and ladder guys—dousing the building from above, working from the elevated aerial basket, probably pushing four or five hundred gallons a minute. The fire, which began on the ground floor, whooshed up the staircase, a natural chimney.

As wet equipment freezes, the guys at the scene are fighting both flames and ice, as though nature has marshaled its most malevolent forces in unholy alliance. The sheer violence of that combination is enough to humble anyone. On this particular evening, giving it everything we've got, we go to the mat with nature—and nature wins, exacting a mortal toll.

Our very best guys (later three will be commended for valor) are in the front door quickly, groping through the smoke and the heat for the victim. They find the old man on the floor, slumped against the kitchen door, overcome before he could escape. He's not a slight load; eight or nine guys help hustle him out of the house and into the waiting Southampton Volunteer ambulance. The ambulance rushes off. The old man never revives.

Not knowing any better, I expected that our department would have experienced such a tragedy maybe every five or six years. Not so, the long-serving guys tell me later. They had pulled people out of burning buildings, they had seen deaths close hand in traffic accidents, but this loss of human life to a blazing fire was the first in memory. Though Chief Corr later described the search team's work as a "good get"—they found and extracted the victim promptly—the death was traumatic for the entire department.

My young friend Paul, part of the search team, also tells me later of groping around the ground floor, crawling, unable to see in the smoke. For a brief time there was a scary report that the old man's sister was also at home when the blaze erupted. On hands and knees, probing with a tool, Paul felt his way into nooks and crannies and corners and under beds. Paul, a new father, was making damn sure his search didn't overlook a child.

Half a block away, I don't learn that sad history until the next day. With one notable exception, it's my job to remain on the far periphery of the fire scene, blocking streets, redirecting traffic, keeping it moving, and protecting the fire ground from intruders, well-meaning or not. (One midnight last month we were nearly knocked down when a woman whipped her car around the corner and up Moses Lane to the fire. "That's my house," the woman cried as she stepped on the gas.)

The only time I get anywhere near a fire is when I help the interior guys change their air tanks. The tanks, worn on a rack and good for no more than twenty minutes, are too cumbersome to remove and replace without help. The fireman stands passively, catching a short break, while we snap open a catch and twist (and twist, and twist) a knob to disconnect the air hose. Then we pop a spring release. Out with the empty tank; in with the new; reverse the process. Twisting that little black knob takes forever. Do it regularly, and it makes for a strong wrist.

Ask a veteran, *What did you do in the war?* and he can tell you that, but little more. Thousands may have died—all he knows is the couple of hundred yards in front of his foxhole. More than a few times I chafe at the frustration of being distant from the real action at a fire scene. Later I tell myself that's how it is with any great cause. For every top dog in the spotlight, thousands of citizens must serve humbly, their gift to their larger community.

What I mainly remember at one remove from that tragic evening when one old man died was the cold, the bitter cold and the biting wind. At ten o'clock, it was about eleven degrees. A northwest wind, twenty miles an hour, give or take, was gusting from Great Peconic Bay a couple of miles away, importing the chill all the way from arctic Canada.

Donny, Dave and I held that intersection for a bit less than an hour and a half. We halted traffic as the pumpers and trucks raced up North Sea and wheeled west up Hillcrest. We closed off Hillcrest with barricades and cones. Now, as we stand shivering, our burden has waned to waving gawkers on past and occasionally opening the barricades for some official vehicle to pass in or out.

I am encased in my day-glow lime green duty jacket with its thick black liner. I never stand stationary, bouncing about like a prizefighter in the ring. As much as I can, I face south along North Sea Road, so the back of my hood takes the brunt of the wind. For all that, I am chilled to the bone. I brought the wrong gloves; my fingers are numb. I can barely hold my flashlight, the yellow heavy-duty one with the lit orange tip, the most visible for directing traffic, day or night. My legs are okay, but my feet have become clumps. Up till now, we've had a mild winter, so I am still in running shoes on this frigid night in late January. After maybe an hour some Samaritan does a coffee-and-cocoa run to the 7-Eleven, a long block away. The cocoa is wonderful. My fingers are so cold, I drop the precious cup after only a sip. The cup blows away, tumbling along North Sea Road toward the village.

My lieutenant Jason yells, "Fred, take a break — go sit in the truck and get warm." The first two times, I shook my head and grinned gamely. What I lack in youth, I will make up in grit. The third time around, I can no longer stand it. The gutter is now slush from the water run-off; trying to skip over, I soak only one shoe, only a bit. My eyes are tearing. When I reach the truck, my fingers won't work the door handle. Once inside, I am bliss. The warmth caresses my cheeks; gloves off, my fingers begin to thaw and flex. But I am antsy, too antsy to shelter for more than five minutes, and then it's back on the street.

All the next day I am groggy. Only then do I realize what a blow the cold had delivered. That hour and a half of exposure wracked me like a full-body concussion. As it happens, I am up early to take the six-thirty Jitney to Manhattan. Something impels me to go see the wound that I experienced only from a distance. I veer my Jeep a couple of blocks out of my way and turn up Hillcrest, peering for the scene of all that action. In the pre-dawn darkness, it's surprisingly hard to locate the right house. The shell of the building still stands. The first time I drive past without recognizing a thing. Turning around, I finally pick out the place. I see the security SUV in the driveway, nesting back in the shadows. I shiver at the sight of the charred, empty home where fire and smoke stole an old man's life.

BJØRN HOLME~

When I lived in Danmark in 1974, environmental awareness was just blossoming in the United States. The first Earth Day had been celebrated just a couple of years earlier, organic food was out there and people were waking up to energy alternatives. I was living on the island of Fynn in a tiny storybook village called Dalby. I lived on an apple farm. I was merely a student who had decided to spend the year in Danmark for an adventure. Little did I know that my adopted family, the Bjorns, were poster children for environmentally friendly living. The experience was the foundation for informing my life. Thirty-four years later sustainability language is everywhere one looks or listens: living simple, reducing one's carbon footprint, reusing, going green. It is all good and so was my summer in Dalby, Danmark.

Anna Bjorn, the matriarch, had great intelligence and energy. I am sure this inspired her to invite American students to her home each summer. She had been doing it for at least ten years by the time I appeared. As a woman in the traditional male-dominated culture, her talents were most likely taken for granted. How hard this must have been for so motivated a person. I believe that she found a way through us, her "charges," to teach and be heard, as she most needed. She had already achieved a high degree of education with a college degree in Home Economics, as well as enjoying a rich talent for classical piano. So it was natural for her to seek more than the routine work of a farmer's wife, no matter how busy that can be. She had the capacity to really do more, and I was blessed to be placed in her care.

The day started early in the Bjorn household. Anna fed her husband Ijvind and his assistant Charles their first meal at 5:00 a.m. She fixed the same thing every morning for them, a gruel made from the leftover thick rye bread we had yesterday. I could smell its yeastiness in my room above, but not being invited down until 8:30 a.m., I never tasted it. Boiled with beer, the crumbled bread filled both men for their early morning rounds in the orchard.

So as she bustled in her kitchen, I looked out my window and saw the rows and rows of apple trees from directly below my windows in their green-leafed and red-dotted harvest outfits. I loved my window at Bjorns. The casement had no screens, so when open it revealed the land and sky without filter. My nose and eyes loved it at any hour day or night. And being in Scandinavia, the nights were long with waning sun until about 11:00 p.m. My table/desk sat right at the window. Letters were written home every day from my view of this magical farm. And despite lingering homesickness, this hardware store owner's daughter grew in awe of her surroundings and the people in them.

Anna's kitchen was a source of great pride to her. She had a large kitchen with a delightful eating nook in one corner. There we shared all three meals each day except on the rare event of company. Then we used the dining room across the hall. The kitchen was bright and sunny and obviously modernized as it contained an electric dishwasher, which Anna did not use all the time. The cabinets were bright yellow and the floor and counter sea blue. Anna walked around that kitchen with authority. This was her domain.

The tiny electric refrigerator took up a cabinet space at eye level on the wall. It contained butter, mayonnaise and small amounts of meat from the freezer. The freezer in the basement held a store of meat, mostly pork, and other preserved foods for the year. The tiny refrigerator was not full, although it was one quarter the size of our family refrigerator in America. The storage room off the kitchen held many of the items we would have found in our own refrigerator in New York. This little room was a cooling room, so eggs and jams and jellies were stored here, as well as leftovers that did not need full refrigeration. Anna made delicious jam from the strawberries that grew under the apple trees right outside the kitchen. Every day we had a wonderful fresh batch to spread on the soft white rolls at breakfast.

At about 8:15 I ventured down to the kitchen. There in the nook was a table waiting to be set with linens. Anna took great pride in her linens. There were special ones with cut lace and embroidery for the dining room. In the kitchen we had soft cotton napkins and a tablecloth with a smart Danish woven design. We each had our own napkin to be used until laundry day. Anna had assigned me my own wooden napkin ring distinguishable by a small design. Each family member or guest got one when sharing a meal at her table. To this day, I follow this tradition, saving hundreds of dollars and wasted energy in paper products. Anna taught me to set the table her way, placing the cutlery just so, as she would approve. Her watchful eye did not miss a fork out of line. She always had a fresh flower or two in a small vase on the table. It was all so civil.

Breakfast was the same each day. Beautiful soft white bread with Danish butter and the strawberry jam. Warm soft-boiled eggs in lovely little egg-cups with hearty rye bread to sop up the yolk. And at each setting was a special tiny glass of precious orange juice for each. Anna was ahead of her time serving this treat to her family. Rich home-ground coffee was served, too. Ijvind joined us with Olav, their son, who was at home for the summer. We all started the meal together at Anna's command: *"Versko og Spise!"* "With pleasure eat!"

ॐContra Dance

"Hands four from the top. Face your neighbor and balance and swing." These instructions come from a dance caller who stands before us on stage at the Concord Scout House in Massachusetts. It is Saturday evening of Thanksgiving weekend 1986. My husband, Eric, and I are visiting his family for the holiday. A chance to get out for the evening brought us here. Grandmother is home with our young daughter. Our host, an old friend, is an avid contra dancer. His enthusiasm has ushered us here. We are game to try it, too.

The Scout House, a mammoth wood-frame community hall, stands in the center of Concord. Its exposed rough rafters and worn wood floors speak to the many who have congregated here over the centuries. Folding chairs line the sides of the hall. Minutes before the caller takes his place, dancers of all ages stream in, hands and eyebrows lifting to greet fellow dancers and the caller.

After paying five dollars at the door, most claim a chair and change into what appears to be serious dance shoes — black leather with laces and thin, soft leather soles. This must indicate a high level of proficiency. Things are getting interesting. How serious could this be? I wonder. How little do I know?

I look around at the other dancers in my line. They are ruddy New Englanders with fresh-air skin, rosy cheeks looking as though they just stepped out of the apple orchard. Most are dressed in no-nonsense well-worn clothes faded in the way that speaks of comfort combined with frugality. Men decked out in soft flannel shirts and jeans and the women in sensible skirts with conservative tops. Current fashion statements of a trendy kind are absent, the closest being some Indian gathered skirts popular on college campuses in the 60s and 70s. Classic wool A-lines predominate. In surprising contrast, I notice a crowd of youngsters and even teens, decked out more in line with MTV, greeting each other with comfortable confidence. I am intrigued by this bridge of generations.

Rife with anticipation, I feel a case of nervous giggles coming on, which I stifle. There are about 75 people of all ages lined up in two long lines. The caller is on the stage above us. Musicians holding fiddles and guitars sit in the same folding chairs at center stage. One sits at a piano to the side. They relax, instruments draped casually across laps, sharing quiet laughs, waiting for the caller to finish instructing us so they can get to work.

We stand in two long lines, partner facing partner, an arm stretch from each other. I glance at Eric with a smile of hopeful excitement. He is desperately trying to focus on the instructions and doesn't even see me. The caller has finished talking us through the pattern of the dance sans music. I realize my feet followed, but my brain has no clue what he taught. We are about to start and, now panicked, I fully realize that there is no escape. What if I totally screw up? Deserting the line now would mean all the dancers would have to reset themselves. We had already formed little circles of four dancers down the line. The shame and embarrassment of fleeing the line weigh more heavily than taking the chance of screwing up.

The music is starting. Abandonment strategies are quickly replaced with pure raw drive for surviving. The music captures my whole being with rhythm and melody rooted in the depths of my Scottish ancestry. A strong piano backup is heard playing, steady chord progression informing every step. It intertwines magically with the melody notes spilling rapidly off the fiddle. Now I am not facing Eric, but instead turned to my neighbor, the other man in our little circle. I look down to check on his shoes. Seeing a flash of black, I silently thank God. We are doing the first vaguely familiar move: "Balance and swing the one below." In the firm embrace of this stranger I flash a nervous smile. He responds, but without the nervous part. There is no pause as the music swells and the next call is given. "Ladies Chain!" With that, my neighbor nudges me toward the center and his partner catches my right hand, pulling me past her toward Eric. Eric as usual looks calm, but the deadpan expression hides the panic of "what the heck is supposed to happen next?" For a brief moment, we fear our separation from the neighbors we came to depend on in the first thirty seconds of the music. "Swing your partner!" I begin to break out in near maniacal laughter. We swing each other, imitating as best we can what we observe others doing. The swing lasts several perfectly timed chord changes by the piano. Instantly, it is over as the caller cries "Chain back!" There is no time to think as I am pulled back across the line to my neighbor, where he whisks me around to stand in the long line facing Eric again. "Forward and Back!" We simply walk four steps forward and four steps back, all in line. The serious black shoes do some fancy stomping as they move to and fro. This encourages the band to amp it up. I have entered the zone of anticipation panic in which my adrenaline keeps me poised to face the next move I can't figure out. "Circle Left!" Holy moly, I know this! This I can do. And with confidence I take my neighbor and Eric's hands as we make a little circle of four all the way 'round. For this brief second of confident clarity I am able to observe something really cool. My neighbor's partner, the other woman in our cozy circle, moves her feet and body with a slight twisting motion in rhythm, inviting her Indian skirt to flow back and forth around her ankles. I want to try that, too. But, alas, the circling is complete. We move on. "Star Right!" With right wrists clasped in each other's hands we form a tightly locked square of hands in the center, around which we move a little more quickly.

The musicians pick up the tempo and some dancers hoot and shout. The dance is in high gear! I am completely charged by the energy of the dance hall. Suddenly, my first familiar neighbor is gone, and a new one faces me to balance and swing all over again. Shoes of all shapes and colors move up and down these old wood floors, swinging, do-si-doing, prome-nading and parading. Repeating this same sequence of moves, we progress down the line with every other couple, finishing each time to face miraculously someone new, who thankfully guides us along.

The caller stopped calling a few rounds back; now it is the dancers who move to the rhythm of the steady piano beat, while the fantastic fiddle tunes of Ireland and Scotland permeate the hall. I am at the mercy of this group of strangers as I complete my first contra dance. It is an intimate encounter with every new face, arm, and hand down the line. Each person, unique and original, is enveloped in the moment of music and movement. A moving tapestry, we weave together through the magic of the dance.

ॐHilary Woodwardॐ

ॐPickle Juice

It is July 4th, 1963, Southampton, New York. I am nine years old. I sit in the back of my father's pickup truck along with an assortment of cousins. Phil, my favorite, sits with me. All the bathing suits, towels, and the picnic stuff are packed. We are headed for "The Tower," a summer family camp high on the bluff above Peconic Bay. Uncle Tom and Aunt Helen are the hosts. Aunt Helen's father built the tower a long time ago. It is so high we can see it from the car way before we get there.

We race toward Shinnecock Canal. Wind is blowing in our faces. We perch against the sides of the back of the pickup. We all want to be the first to spot the tower. The peek is visible just over the tall pine trees that surround it right off the road. Everyone has eyes peeled on the landscape ahead.

Suddenly, a flash of white flies out of the back of the truck. What is that? It looks like underwear! It is! They belong to Philip. We all laugh. Philip does, too. We laugh for the rest of the ride, thinking about someone finding Philip's underwear. Just as quickly my older sister yells "I see the tower!" We all look to see it grow larger on approach. Finally we arrive.

Our parents unload all the picnic supplies along with the other parents. There must be about 10 or 12 families here. Uncle Tom has gotten a large grill going. There are wooden slat hammocks slung between the trees. Each family settles on a spot among the pine trees. Ours has a big blanket and a couple of wooden back rests for grandparents. Metal camp tables are set up, too. These are for the potluck. Baked beans, potato salads and casseroles are placed there. Pickles, mustard, ketchup, relish, and hamburger rolls and buns complete the feast.

The parents tell us kids to start toward the changing shacks to change into our bathing suits. "Don't touch the poison ivy!" we hear as we start down the path toward the bay. The wooden stall that stands off the path frightens me. The wood is old and faded. Worse, there are spiders inside. My mother has caught up to me. She says they won't bite. We hurry into our suits. "Don't touch the poison ivy" again on the way to the beach. We come to the edge of the bluff. There are already others on the beach and in the bay. My grandfather, Gaku, is here. Oh! Philip has already gotten to the beach. He is playing with Peter in the water. Tommy and his cousins have brought a sailboat. They are out further than I am allowed to go. I want to race down, but am stuck behind my mom on the steep narrow steps.

On the beach, I run and dive into the water. I am so excited to join the kids on the float. It is the most fun. We dive off over and over. We practice our dives and then compete to see who gets the best score. My dad and Gaku, floating nearby, judge. I get an 8, almost perfect, just a small splash on entry. Peter, Philip, and Billy are all doing cannonballs. They make so much noise. I do one, too. I love to play with the boys.

Gaku, standing chest deep in the water, has been digging clams with his toes. He drags an inner tub with a bushel basket tucked inside. We decide to help and dive down to the bottom to retrieve a clam next to his foot. I am too big to jump off his shoulders anymore. He smiles and laughs as we surface with big chowder clams for the basket. He taught me to swim here when I was five. By holding me on his forearms like a tray, I learned to float face up in the water first. After that, I knew I could always float if I were in trouble in the water. I love floating. I watch the sky and feel peaceful.

The parents have started to call us out of the water. "Lunch time! Time to get out! Come on, hurry-up." Everyone is climbing back up. Our parents turn to call again. Now we are all out. Wrapped in towels, fingers crinkled from water, we follow to the pine grove. FOOD! Uncle Tom has grilled a hundred hot dogs. He places them on rolls and sends us off to add the fixins. I love ketchup and relish. Pickles, too, on the side of my plate and a heap of creamy white potato salad with just a bit of parsley for color. The first bite pops the hot dog skin; a bit of dog juice squirts onto my tongue. My taste buds cheer. Auntie Alma's oatmeal bread with a big dollop of softened butter can't be left out. Grandmother's brownies are passed. I pick the biggest, center cut where they are the fudgiest.

Now the parents start to settle in to talk and rest. They take control of the hammocks and the blankets. We kids start to play in and around the tower. We climb wooden ladders inside the tower to the top, passing two floors, each narrower than the last and each jammed with bunk beds.

Soon we want to go in the bay and ask if we can. "In one hour. You must wait an hour before swimming or you can drown." That is always the same answer! We ask again. "Forty-five minutes." Time drags. Parents talk, laugh and rest. We get restless.

After a bit, Phil and I find ourselves at the camp table. We help ourselves to another pickle. He dares me to drink some of the juice. I do and then dare him. He does, too. We start to take turns swigging from the bottle. It tastes sour and sweet, like the pickles! After a bit we stop. We ask again, "How long?" Fifteen minutes to go. Yay! We can go back in the water in 15 minutes.

But no, wait a minute. Uncle John tells us we need to wait for another hour because we have been drinking pickle juice. "It can be a problem for swimmers." What? I can't believe it. "Another whole hour?" we ask. "It is very serious." I get a lump in my throat and my lower lip trembles. Just as quick, all the parents start to laugh. The joke is on Phil and me. I don't think it is so funny. The day has turned a bit sour just like the pickles. I bow my head and feel my chest sink as they laugh at me.

"Times up, back in the bay," the parents announce. Phil and I look at each other and start toward the path.

"Watch out for the poison ivy," my mother calls out as we disappear around it.

≫Hilary Woodward≪

≫Heart Opener

I stand on the city curb where Loie, my best friend, will fetch me for an overnight visit. It is Boston in January: freezing cold, blustery winds and sun. Across the street I watch people emerge from the Prudential Center. They carry deluxe shopping bags and some pull roll-on luggage, too. Above them is the glass skywalk connecting high-end stores and hotels in the sprawling convention center complex. Everyone walks with purpose. None stand around.

I, too, have just emerged from the convention center. I came to the city to attend a yoga workshop in the Sheraton all morning. The theme of the session was "Opening the Heart." From head to heart to toes every part of my 55-year-old self feels released and revived from the intense three-hour practice. Enveloped in my down jacket, knit cap, cashmere scarf and huge down mittens, I won't be catching my "death" even though damp clothes stick to my sweaty frame. Despite city fumes, the bracing air refreshes me. It brings a tingle to my skin. I decide to wait outside.

I look down at my hiking boots. They are completely scuffed. The once rich brown leather is close to the dull gray of the pavement. I pulled them from the back of my closet yesterday, thinking that they would be comfortable and practical for navigating the snowy city. My pants are Capri-length knit, gray, also. I must look a bit like a country bumpkin or hobo with old leather hikers and the cropped pants that don't meet, thus leaving my lower legs exposed. Luckily, I shaved my legs this morning. I have on a black knitted baseball-style cap that can pull way down over my forehead and neck. It has a logo in bright stitching to which my daughter offered, "Cool, Mom." I feel hip from the neck up, anyway.

Directly behind me is the Back Bay train station. I turn to observe the scene. There are hangers-on here, people who have time to stand. A few student types look at a map, a man in a suit checks his watch, a Hispanic mother emerges from large revolving doors, Spanish words admonishing the young child whose mittened hand she clutches.

One man catches my attention. He stands directly behind me. I try not to stare but take in the gist of his situation. He holds a sign. It reads "help the homeless" and has a cup attached at the bottom. He is tall and robust. I guess he must be in his sixties. Gray hair peeks out from a wool cap, gray beard neatly trimmed against his jaw. His winter coat old but clean. His shoes look good and appropriate for the temperature. Nearby stands the kind of wire cart one sees old women pull behind them to the grocery store. It is filled with clothes and plastic bags. They are not jumbled, but have order. I assume it is his. He stands against a pillar, sign held directly in front of his chest. He has pride, I conclude.

I wonder how long he has been there. Does anyone ever stop to give anything to these people who are scattered all over? How much does he make in a day? Is he really homeless or is this just a scam? He looks too good for my image of the homeless. I catch myself and decide that no matter what his situation, he is at heart a fellow human in need. Even if this is a "shtick," he no doubt is trying to get by.

Should I give him something? Here I stand, hobo, yoga self, waiting for a ride to a warm home with good food and clean sheets. I think of my grandmother, who gave food to those who knocked at her back door for help. She believed in giving nourishment, rather than cash that could be spent on alcohol. What can I offer?

I look down at my rolling carry-on bag. On top of it rests my yoga mat, rolled and held together with a canvas strap. It could pass for a bedroll. The canvas strap slung over the pull handle keeps the yoga mat secure. I don't have a purse. All my possessions for this weekend are tightly packed and bundled at my feet. I remember the giant mitsu apple bought from the local orchard yesterday. It is in there somewhere.

A car pulls up. It is an economy-style, compact station wagon, like our old Saturn. In the front sits a couple. They are black and middle aged. Behind them the car is packed to the gills with all kinds of stuff, including some small pieces of furniture. I wonder if they, too, have all their possessions with them. The man steps out of the driver's side. He is humongous, with a grin to match stretched across his broad face.

He looks me up and down and asks, still grinning, "Did you run away from home?"

Taken aback a bit, I smile, answering "No" with a slight laugh.

He laughs and makes his way into the station. Do I really pass for a runaway, or was he kidding? His partner looks out at me. Her hair is neatly coiffed, her face made up simply. She stares at my feet.

My cell phone rings. Loie is across the street, her Volvo idling. I quickly reach into my roll-on and grab the apple. Turning, I offer it to the homeless man. His face, delighted, brightens. "Thank you!" with an emphasis on thank in a strong eastern European accent. I return a smile, and for a moment we link smile to smile, eyes to eyes, heart to heart. Crossing the street, I exhale a huge breath. Hopping in beside Loie, I ask, "Do you have shoe polish at home?"

✎ Margaret Kobalka ✎

The Jacket ✎

I bought the jacket at an Army Navy store—a khaki-colored safari jacket, with epaulets and back vent, belted, with button flaps over the four front patch pockets. The bottom pockets—like kangaroo pouches, expanding to hold (perhaps) a map, a compass, a Swiss Army Knife for a past soldier—held my essentials: keys, tissues, a hair band, a lip gloss and money. The jacket was too long and large on me. I took up the hem and cinched the belt tight in a knot, letting the buckle swing freely in front. I wore the jacket with a tee shirt, hip-hugger jeans, sandals or brown suede moccasins I bought in Greenwich Village. I wore aviator sunglasses and love beads.

It was the uniform of the 1960s—an anti–Vietnam War statement made with a military jacket from another war. It articulated a political view that might incite confrontation or invite comradery. It was the uniform of a new army: the Anti-Establishment. There were debates and rallies. There was name-calling: un-American, Hippie, Flower Child and worse. Someone said the F.B.I. was taking our photographs. But my most vivid memory of the jacket was wearing it on a Sunday afternoon, not to a protest march, but to a "Love-In" at Central Park. I have a photograph someone took of me with my boyfriend, his arm draped over my shoulder. It was a day when people floated and everyone got along. The peace and love message evaporated later that day when I failed to appear, as expected by my Italian father, for Sunday afternoon dinner—just as his father had expected him.

In retrospect my jacket may have signaled rebellion on more than one home-front issue, but eventually I had no need to wear my political views and Sunday traditions prevailed. The jacket lost prominence in my wardrobe, replaced by others, more feminine and fashionable. I almost threw it out once, but retrieved it from a box of discarded clothing before the garbage was taken away.

I still have my army jacket. Occasionally I try it on, amazed that it is no longer too large or too long. I can still button the jacket, but the back vent doesn't lie flat. At some point I restored the original length, but there is a permanent line marking where I folded the hem. While studying the fit in the mirror I resolve to wear it again, but I never do. Now I have other safari jackets, ones with brand-name labels. I hang the old one next to them in the closet and close the door.

ॐMargaret Kobalkaॐ

A Day in the
Park with Sethॐ

Seconds after I lift you out of the stroller and your feet touch the ground, you're racing through Fort Tryon Park. Your laughter, carried on the breeze, floats toward me as I follow. You are the explorer. I am the safety net, ready to scoop you up and away from danger. Your father is there, photographing your actions, capturing motion.

Long, brown, wavy hair flying as you run, the dark-blue polo shirt quickly working its way out of the waistband of your pants. The shirt barely covers your round belly. The new cream color pants, legs turned up at the bottoms, already have dirt and grass stains on the knees. You run fast, even in those two-tone brown leather oxfords. You need sneakers now, but you're growing so fast, and we can't afford both. Anyway, "hard-sided shoes are better for growing feet," the shoe salesman assured me.

You pause, arms and legs still. You bite your lip and roll your big hazel eyes upward to the left, a sign you are planning your next move. Off you go to the carved stone water fountain. Standing on the small stone step, you raise yourself up, spread your fingers on the metal dome and push the button down with all your three-year-old strength. The water spurts up in a high arch. After a drink you hold water in your mouth until your cheeks puff out and water dribbles down your chin.

Bicyclists are waiting by the fountain for their turn, so you go to the stroller to get your "pipe." Holding the stem of the black and yellow miniature pipe up to your mouth you puff pretend smoke, imitating Grandpa Joe. The gap between your baby teeth is visible when you open your mouth, and there is a scratch across your right cheek. Not a cat scratch, probably an accidental one, while playing with your cousin.

Time to go. I push the empty stroller. You stop on the wide walkway and stand on a manhole cover. Bent at the waist, arms propelled up and back, you peer down. Curiosity satisfied, we walk home.

۶Margaret Kobalka

۶Living on the Edge

We have come post-storm to comb the beach for treasures churned up from the depths of the sea by a late autumn storm. My husband and I are surprised to see the dunes are gone, swept away by the winds and waves. We gape at the private walkway steps, nestled for decades behind the dunes, now dangling over sand cliffs. We wander the beach, pointing out the newly formed sandbars and tidal pools, remarking how wide the beach has become. Paul shows me concentric circle patterns etched in the sand by wind-blown ribbons of seaweed. The seagulls take flight, shrieking as they dive and circle, then drop their legs like landing gear and float effortlessly on air currents down to the sandbars.

Paul begins the hunt while I walk. I find a level stretch near the water between tire tracks left in the sand by an early morning driver. Gauging a straight path to a distant point, I close my eyes. Silently counting my steps, I walk forward, cutting the air with my body the way a boat cuts through water. I smell the sea and taste salt deposited on my lips by the wind. I press my fingers to my ears, muffling the sound of the waves, then release the pressure to hear the surf crash against the shore with its promise and warning. Stretching out my arms, my skin feels electrified. I almost understand the mystifying cries of the gulls.

Opening my eyes, I see that Paul and I have kept a parallel pace. We have stopped at the same point, as if connected by an invisible axle. He walks toward me, his hands overflowing with shells, stones and sea glass stacked in clamshells. Holding them up, close to my eyes, I examine each one as it is offered.

✒Margaret Kobalka✑

Accessory Witness✑

My friend and I had been shopping on a side street in Sag Harbor when we noticed postcards in a plastic holder outside a storefront yoga studio. While I looked at the schedule of classes and the styles of yoga instruction listed on the postcard, Adrienne encouraged me, "You should take a class. Do you want to go inside?"

"Hmm, I don't know," I said, "I'm not really a joiner kind of person."

She pressed on, "You'll enjoy it...be good for you... relaxing." Her voice trailed off as I became distracted by a pair of clogs left by the doorway.

"Why would someone leave their shoes here?" I asked.

My question hung in the air as the door to the studio opened. Two women, barefooted and wearing yoga outfits, stood in the doorway. The inner air smelled of incense. Mauve and burgundy gauze privacy curtains caught the open-door draft and fluttered in the room. One woman stepped outside and into the clogs. She smiled serenely at me, and I watched her walk across the street.

The other woman noticed the card in my hand. "If you have any questions," she said, "I'll be happy to help."

I was still watching the clog-wearing woman walk away but managed to say, "Thanks, I'm thinking about taking classes, I'll call." She, too, emanated serenity with a smile and closed the door with a quiet, fluid motion.

Adrienne and I window-shopped and chatted about what else we would do the next few days during her visit. We walked along the wharf and took photos of each other in front of millionaires' yachts docked at the marina. I was still thinking about the clogs on the doorstep.

"I couldn't leave my shoes outside like that. If I had to leave my shoes outside, I'd think about them the entire class and worry about someone taking them." Adrienne suggested I could wear a really worn out pair of shoes. I pictured my old pair of shoes plucked up by a passing Good Samaritan who, thinking them thoughtlessly abandoned but still serviceable, would bring them two doors down to the thrift shop.

People in foreign countries leave their shoes outside their hotel rooms at night to be shined. I couldn't do it. How could I sleep wondering if the shoe shiner would get mine mixed up with someone else's shoes? I made a mental note to write my initials in my shoes, just in case I had to prove, at some later date, they were mine.

"Or," Adrienne said, "You could put your shoes in your bag during class."

"Bag? What bag? She didn't have a bag either. What kind of woman doesn't carry a handbag?"

I scanned the crowded wharf for bagless clog-wearing women, but found none.

I felt an opportunity had slipped through my hands to meet the one person among the throngs of accessory-obsessed people who had successfully detached from them. I had questions I needed her to answer. Yoga pants have no pockets. Where's her stuff? Where are her keys? Does she leave her car and house doors unlocked? Could a woman really not carry a lipstick and tissues, a wallet, ID, money, credit and library cards, photos and all the other tons of stuff women cram into the shoulder bags that wreck rotator cuffs?

Afterwards, I became hyper-observant about people's cavalier treatment of their things. I was on accessory patrol. The unchained bicycle outside the post office with the helmet balanced on the seat. The Mercedes convertible parked with the top down at the beach with expensive sunglasses on the seat and no owner in sight. All kinds of paraphernalia scattered on vacant towels, while people were in the water or strolling the beach. When I admonished a woman in the grocery store for leaving her handbag unattended in her cart, I knew my vigilance was getting out of hand. I needed to get away, to relax, to let it all go. I went to visit Adrienne (the voice of reason) in Hartsdale for a few days.

So it's Passover and also the Sunday of Pope Benedict's mass at Yankee Stadium. The Dalai Lama has recently been in the U.S. With so many religious and spiritual events, it seems a good day for a pilgrimage.

Although Adrienne and I are both Catholic, we're interested in meditation, so we drive to the Chuang Yen Monastery in Carmel. The temple houses a 37-foot porcelain statue of the Buddha, the largest Buddha in the western hemisphere, and I want to see it.

From the parking lot we see the Great Hall, with its Chinese Dynasty architecture. We have traveled to China the easy way; we laugh and head towards a wide, light-colored, stone tile walkway that leads uphill towards the temple. The walk is flanked on both sides by white statues with various facial expressions and poses. One statue's face is frozen in a scream; another cradles the side of his head with a hand. There's a statue with a snarling guard dog beside it; others have expressions of contentment.

Adrienne thinks the uphill path is the ascent to "heaven" and the statues represent people encountered in life. We slow our pace, continue our procession and whisper to each other about the statues. The quality of the air begins to change; it feels pure. We breathe deeply.

Most of the people along the path look Asian. They nod at us and smile slightly as we pass. Drum and bell towers are at the top of the hill to either side of the temple. We climb steep, gray, pyramid-like stone stairs to the Great Buddha Hall.

There are lit incense sticks in a large, sand-filled bowl on a table under the red-roof overhang at the top of the stairs. A woman lights a stick of incense, using one from the bowl. A stream of jasmine-scented smoke rises into the air, and I wonder if the woman has said a prayer or has made a request.

As we approach the double doors of the temple, I notice a sign, point to it and whisper to Adrienne, "The sign says 'Take off your shoes before entering.' " My friend gives me a look that I know means, "Can you do it?" She suggests we go in separately if I'm concerned about leaving my shoes outside.

I watch people enter the temple after quickly removing their shoes and leaving them on the porch or in a wooden cubicle that looks like the ones in bowling alleys. Numbers are still attached to some of the cubbies. Adrienne removes her sneakers and places them in a cubby. As the doors to the temple swing open and closed, I catch a glimpse of the Great Buddha perched atop an enormous white lotus flower, in the cavernous hall with its high-arched beams. I slip off my brand-new, size 6, seventy-nine-dollar shoes and place them on a shelf next to Adrienne's larger-sized sneakers. I'm going in! But before I do, I lean against Adrienne, tap her sneakers and whisper to them, "Watch over my shoes." Then I open the door and enter the temple with newfound faith.

꙳Joan M. Mazzu꙳

If I Could
Talk to My Mother꙳

I would tell you that old age is like basking in a warm pool, not like a young swimmer slapping in the ocean. I wish you had not missed the sweet stream of the journey.

How old was I when you told me about the pansy faces? It is almost spring here and time for pots of nodding purple, blue and yellow pansies waiting to go home.

I have passed on the story to your granddaughters and great-granddaughters, that each pansy has a different face and each one is beautiful. I look for you in all of them. None of them has your serene beauty, but there are subtle things. Some are good at math, others so ambitious, all with billowing compassion and no eating raisins in the cake or bread.

꙳   ꙳

I tell them stories about you, Lillian Beaumont Tyler-McKee. How I loved the winter coat with the little beaver collar so much that you found me a little beaver muff to go with it. I tell them about "the measles doll house," and the surprise puppy. I do not tell them that your life was sad. You and Dad, like tall trees sheltering a sapling—different trees not meant to grow together. I do not tell them about the married Lillian.

All that time ago in your house, that was now my house, the climate was bleak and dark for me because you had died. Tea cups, books, prints, bracelets, pillow cases, pots all made me mad that they should exist and you were gone. In your bedroom I found "the girdle" hung on a hook. Like a suit of armor, long, pink, with torturous stays and a zipper on the side, garters dangling empty and clicking. I held it and smelled your scent. I remembered you then younger, healthy, all suited up like a goddess going to war in the field of men. Brave.

๑Joan M. Mazzu๑

Buyer's Remorse๑

There she is again, perfect makeup, perfect hair, amazing square, white-tipped fingernails. The sort of fingernails that defy pot-cleaning or scrubbing. Her perfection is possible because of a crew of makeup artists, hairdressers and wardrobe people.

Her in-front-of-the-camera enthusiasm and persona is all her own. She is excited, jubilant, and wide-eyed as she tells me I must buy the white man-tailored shirt.

"Wear the collar up or down, tuck it in or be casual untucked. Button it all the way up to your neck and be demure, unbutton and show a bit of cleavage." Pam will wink and smile, telling us that a plain white man-tailored shirt can be sexy and naughty too. As time and shirts run out, the excitement grows. "Only a hundred left in XL. We won't have these shirts again until next year." I feel most anxious even though I am not going to buy the shirt. Of the hundreds of white man-tailored shirts out there, is this the one to buy?

I want to know how they do it. Maybe having long, tan fingers with the perfect manicure causes Pam's hysteria about the bottle-cap-sized ring with the very bright stones. She tells us, "Yes, you can wear this ring and the matching earrings with the casual black, green or purple velour sweatsuit that you were smart enough to order in the previous hour." Pam is nice enough then to tell us all of the places we can wear the suit and jewelry.

"Look great for girl's night out, or for casual shopping. You can look put together picking up the kids from school! Just right for the neighbors' barbecue, not to mention holiday parties and that special night out with hubby!" Then a big-lashed wink. Pam is trying to make me feel embarrassed slumping around in a worn grey sweatsuit, hiding behind big sunglasses at King Kullen.

If you order clothes from a catalogue, do they give you such timely hints? No, they just want the numbers in the blue box and the pink box There are no social clues or accessorizing hints at T.J. Maxx, Macy's or Nordstrom.

My fascination with the shopping networks isn't really what they are selling, but how they do it. They reel through a selling mix of options—gentle persuasion, customer endorse-ments, even scolding and exclusion. Do you want to be left out, be un-trendy or, worse, wear an inferior white shirt? Where do these performer-salesladies come from? It is astounding, their exuberance over plain white shirts. Is there a school for TV selling? Do they have to audition? Is there special training? Is it something they drink before they go on?

I have succumbed and ordered just twice. Late one night I ordered a trampoline. Sleep deprived, I forgot that my left knee is sometimes unbending and cranky. The trampoline came and my husband put it together in our bedroom. It was huge and black. I stepped on and did two bounces. I realized that I would be permanently handicapped if I took another bounce.

They took it back without a question. My husband was kind enough not to speak about it again. I also ordered a twenty-four-dollar sewing machine that is still in the box. Waiting for a garage sale.

I do still enjoy the dazzling salesladies, but remem-bering the trampoline I resist the lifetime guarantee cookware, seeded flower mats for an instant garden, garish jewelry, electronic gadgets (most tempting), and much more. Why do I watch? The reality is that I want to be one of those happy, giddy, helpful TV ladies.

❦Joan M. Mazzu❧

Rewrite❧

When my youngest daughter was in high school I gave her $15.00 to recopy our address book. I was distracted and thought she was the organized daughter, the one with the legible handwriting; but no, she was the one who hated tuna fish. Halfway through I checked. She was copying with a magic marker, the names and addresses squeezed in on the tiny lines, the phone numbers resembling ink blot tests. She is now 36, has not given me a refund, and we still use the old book.

My husband and I are at a standoff about a re-copy. "You have neat, small handwriting and are so much better at important details than I am," I tell him.

He doesn't fall for it, just says, "You know what should be included."

"My handwriting is scattered and too big for a phone book," I say

He shakes his head. It's the end of discussion. I have lost again.

There is a rubber band around the wrinkled, black plastic cover; this holds in lists and loose notes. There is a list of real estate agents with my scrawled comments. One says "showed house in pajamas." Another note: "she is so dumb her name should be brick," and so on. Another list, neat and on a small piece of paper at the top of page, says "Golf," then "Joe M," "Joe A," and "Joe T," with phone numbers. Some years ago my husband played golf with three guys, all named Joe. I know nothing about them at all since golfers do not discuss anything but golf. Sideways on another page is a note "sleepover at Tina's" with a phone number next to it that says "nice wine brought by Fran for dinner." The name of the wine smudged. What year, I couldn't possibly guess.

Now some pages have web sites tucked in. Next to epicurious.com are measurements for curtains. What house? In the book "NC" means moved to North Carolina and "D" means dead; I don't like to cross out names. There are many entries under H for handyman and under P for plumbers and pipes. These helpers could be anywhere, no area codes to tell what county or town they are in should we need to call. The other day I tried to retrace and remember the era or connection for the note "yellow house on the corner — turn right for Suzie's." I'm thinking now that in trying to decode these clues we might be helped in deferring dementia, senility, senior moments or whatever the popular term is now for memory loss. My husband says that our phone book is more challenging than Sudoku.

⋟Joan M. Mazzu⋞

A Thousand Women⋞

Who were those women, the thousand — and many thousands? Years of women bearing children. Passing down through the ages their genes for stamina, hair color, and temperament. Were some of my ancestor-sisters priests or chiefs in their clans? Old history tells us that Celtic women had status and say about their lives until organized religion diminished the power and voice of women.

In the year 1000 did the mother of all my mothers realize that the Dark Ages were ending and that the age of light was beginning? Would that be a time of renaissance and light for her? Possibly one of these ancient females waited by the sea for Leif Erickson to return from his discoveries. Is that old gene the one that tells me that I must live near the sea, but have no need to be on the sea?

How sad if one or some of those "before-me-women" were desperate peasants living in murky forests married and bearing children when they were still children. Frightened by warring bands of young thug-like noblemen. They must have been brave to survive and to make sure that their children lived.

In those dark times all but a few were always hungry, and some owed 100 days of labor to the lord for the right to grow a few vegetables. They may have been too busy in their short lives to think of a different world. I think that they did dream, and that dreams helped them to survive

Brigid or Brig, a woman that appears in Celtic mythology and later on as a Christian saint, was said to have made the whistle. She would whistle in the dark to warn others of danger. A small thing but, as the story goes, Brigid saved many lives with her whistle. Smarter than swords and sentries?

In 1002 Brian Boru became High King of Ireland and brought about a rebirth of culture and grace. Was one of my mothers there to sing and tell stories with him? For thousands of years no one knew what songs women wrote and sang or what revolutions they envisioned or plotted.

Maybe an ancestor female sat with other family women and complained about sons, brothers, or husbands going off to fight in the Crusades. She must have been wise enough to suspect that the Crusades were not really about religion, but about power and money for kings and popes. The ancient mothers must have been crafty to keep secret thoughts from men.

Even earlier, did one of my mothers camp outside the hills of Rome and watch her Celtic males strip naked, paint themselves blue and run screaming down the hills to terrify the Romans? Was it her formula for beer that later became so loved by the Romans?

Did some ancient matriarch make tuneless non-melodic humming sounds when she was concentrating? Did she squint in the firelight at scratchings on the wall and imagine books? Do I have the "hate-the-dark gene" from her?

Of course, I shall never know anything of these women. I do know that they were strong, clever and determined to survive. Even the tiniest image of their lives reminds me to find joy in my comfortable days.

ॐJoan M. Mazzuॐ

The Orange Catॐ

Sometimes I see him there, his tail sticking up like a fuzzy orange periscope sailing slowly in back of the hydrangeas. He is an expert stalker, or so he thinks. In the early spring before the bushes bloomed, he would lie flat-out in the baby grass, his nose inches away from the long pole that held the three-family birdhouse.

From the deck I see him flicking his yellow eyes up at the frantic housekeeping birds. Usually he avoids me even though he lives under the deck. Occasionally he does his haughty runway walk past me as I stand at the potting bench.

"Don't you know that you look like a big orange bath mat lying out there like that? You can be seen from everywhere; even the birds next door can see you."

Orange cat gives me a sideways yellow look that says, "How many birds have you caught?"

Possibly he thinks, if he is visible enough, that the birdhouse tenants and the mob living in the three big cedars will stop sounding alarms every time they spot him. I know he is around, even when I'm in the house with the windows closed, by the terrified chirps and calls.

The orange cat doesn't belong to anyone; he is a feral cat, part of a pack that lives in the surrounding woods. My cousin and her husband live two houses away and feed these cats winter and summer. Over the years they have reduced the pack from eight or nine cats to four or five now. Taking a lot of time and trouble, they would catch a mother cat and her babies, have them neutered, then return them to the woods.

As the pack has been reduced I have been able to add a few new birdhouses and another bird bath. The big male orange cat belongs to the third or fourth generation of feral cats; cats in the wild do not live long.

His orange fur is long and fluffy, his tail is wide, and he can switch the end of it in a threatening or annoyed way. One ear is folded like an envelope, a badge from an old battle perhaps. His options are in his eyes. He does his tail-switching thing when he sees me and that is not often; we avoid each other.

The other day when I opened the front door I saw a swish of orange disappear from the bottom of the porch steps. Puzzled, I looked around and discovered that a silly house wren was building her nest in the planter right next to the front door. I had to discourage her by moving the planter. I know the orange cat is serious about killing. His disposition is cantankerous, and my cousin tells me that he fights and bullies the other cats, wanting all the food for himself.

The same day he ran off from stalking the front porch wren, I spotted him depositing cat poop on a hill of composted soil near the edge of the woods. I shouted, and he uttered a cat curse back at me as he ran off—a yowl that surprised me. I had never heard him say anything. I scattered mothballs around the hill of soil, probably not necessary since he seemed so embarrassed.

He was there the other night when I went to close the blinds on the patio doors; he had something in his mouth that was dead. A mole or a mouse, maybe a chipmunk—something long-tailed and dead. He dropped it, then sat and looked at me. I made shooing motions from behind the door; he picked up the tiny body and ran off.

The orange cat no longer sleeps under the deck, and my cousin hasn't seen him for meals. He has decided not to be dependent, to be divorced. Today I saw him in the woods whipping a snake around in his mouth to kill it.

ꝏMary O'Brienꝏ

TURNIPS 3 for $1ꝏ

I don't even like turnips, but the hand-painted sign on the road made me whip my head around to look down the driveway. I had been admiring the farm as we descended the long hill that went past it. I could see a house set way back, a classic, white farmhouse adorned with green shutters and a black-shingled roof, partially hidden by a towering beech. Alongside the road stretched a fallow field with long rows of Brussels sprout stubs left by the harvesters. A long ribbon of unpaved driveway skirted the field and led up to the yard with the house on the left and the small produce stand, just a glorified tabletop actually, on the right. The driveway continued further on towards the hills that edged the narrow valley floor and ended at last at the largest barn I have ever seen, the main bay maybe four stories high. On the gable end were a pair of massive sliding doors, and as we drew closer, I noticed one was slid open. The highly buffed, white body of a 50s-era Rolls Royce Silver Dawn sparkled from within the darkness, incongruous parked next to a red Farmall tractor.

"Bob, go back. Did you see that sign for turnips?"

"Turnips? No, I didn't see any sign." No surprise there; I wonder if he saw the house. Did you ever hear the joke about how it's easier to turn an aircraft carrier around than it is to get a man to go back to look at an interesting thing along the road?

We had spent the day sightseeing around the Annapolis Valley of Nova Scotia. The fertile soil of the ninety-mile valley is filled with farms, making up the only part of Nova Scotia that is not covered with rocks and fir trees. After the past week, I had seen enough picturesque rocks to last awhile, so was comforted to find this valley that looked so much like eastern Long Island.

By only mentioning the turnips I had greatly simplified, but food is Bob's passion. Now I had his attention, but still had to convince him that it would be fun to bring home fresh, local produce. And at the low price of one dollar (Canadian), it would make a great story when we served it in two weeks for Thanksgiving. "And," I added, "I think I saw a vintage Rolls Royce." He turned the car.

There were only a couple turnips left. The farm wife appeared from the side door, buttoning up her hastily thrown-on cardigan, then patting a bit of her snowy white hair back into place. "Don't bother with those few. They've been sitting all afternoon. I'll send my husband up to the field to get some fresh ones," she said, as she turned to go back in the house.

"Hey. Don't bother. These three will be plenty for us," I quickly called her back. "We just want a couple to bring back home."

I guess our accents gave us away. "Ah, you're Americans. My husband will be so delighted to talk to you."

Nothing would do but that we had to come in and meet her husband. No protestations, including that we could not leave the dog in the car alone, had any effect.

Soon we found ourselves comfortably ensconced in a pair of side-by-side upholstered chairs next to the wood stove in the kitchen. Our hostess had hastily scooped an afghan off the settee and arranged it in front of the stove for our Jack Russell, who now was happily gnawing a hambone in her new bed. Our hostess bustled between the kitchen, where she was preparing tea, and the staircase. Every other minute she called up to her husband, requesting that he come down to meet "The Americans" who had come to visit. (Come to visit?) Finally she turned to us. "Deaf as a post," she mouthed, and with great exasperation went upstairs.

A moment later the farmer presented himself. It was as if he had walked out of a Jane Austen novel, the perfect English gentleman-farmer. Tall, jovial, with a florid complexion and a tweed coat, the eightyish man gurgled at us, "Delighted to have you, love company, don't get a lot of Americans up this way, lovely dog you have there, have some tea, ay," as he pulled up another chair to chat.

The farmwife plunked a small table between us and finished setting out the tea, little sandwiches and cakes, then hung up her flowered apron before joining us. I relaxed deeper into my chair and enjoyed the warm fire as I sipped the strong Canadian tea. I'd had this Red Rose tea before, brought down by Bob's visiting Nova Scotia in-laws. It was not the same Red Rose that I usually purchased in the A&P. The Canadians tease me that my Red Rose is only fit for garden parties or wimpy Americans. Their Red Rose produced the pot of tea that got the farmers and fishermen in this cold province through their hard-work lives.

We talked of one thing and another—the weather, the crops: his produce, ours potatoes. Then I mentioned, "You have a beautiful barn out there." It was as if I had uttered the magic word. The farmer and his wife sprang to the edge of their chairs. Their hands fluttered and their eyes took on a glistening shine as they excitedly told us about the storm.

"It hit late in the summer while we were harvesting," he said. "It was fierce."

She took over. "First we got the end of Danielle, then a bit of Earl. That was nothing. We've had hurricanes before, and these were mostly spent, but then they merged and they battered Nova Scotia."

"...the rains were teeming. The winds, blowing a gale," he threw in. They interrupted each other in their zeal to make sure we understood just how ferocious a tempest it had been. "The rains kept battering the roof...and the wind. The wind roaring up the valley. All these windows rattled, and we were terrified they'd be ripped out. We couldn't keep it out. That cruel wind pushed right under the shingles into the house."

"And then," she almost whispered, "a ferocious buster hit the barn like a fist. That barn's been standing there for a hundred or more years but that night, over it went."

"But the barn is standing," Bob said, wonderingly. The farmer's wife picked up the teapot and refilled each cup. The cake plate was passed around, and I saw from the farmer's expression that the best part of the tale was coming up. I settled back in my chair.

"They all came. They all came from the farms on their machines."

His wife clarified, "The neighbors. They all drove over on their tractors."

"They lined 'em up on the north side there, and we swung some line over to each. On the word, they all pulled, and that barn popped right back up." Seeing our disbelieving faces, he added, "That barn was built by my grandfather. It's all one piece. Peg and beam. All the beams are mortised together."

As the tea things were cleared away, his wife said they had plenty of room, would we stay. The farmer echoed her. Bob said we had a reservation at a hotel in town. Prepaid. We really had nowhere to go, but tea with absolute strangers seemed daring enough. We were too shy to stay the night.

On the ferry back to Maine I was running over in my mind how I'd tell this story while passing the bowl of steaming turnips this Thanksgiving, and suddenly I remembered. I never did get around to asking about the Rolls Royce. Or their names.

❧Mary O'Brien❧

A Drawstring Apron❧

All week I had been practicing my catwalk stride and half turns until I could do it like any seasoned beauty queen. My mother had set my hair and I looked great, except for my glasses, but everyone said I had to wear them or I would get lost during my turn on stage.

Our MC was to be Edgar Bergen, then famous for his ventriloquist show with Charlie McCarthy, now more well known as Candice Bergen's father. The fashion show was being held in the big auditorium of a huge, newly built suburban high school. The stage was intimidatingly enormous, and all the twelve-year-olds nervously huddled behind the curtain, peeking out at the crowds as they began to find their seats.

The older girls, veterans of these events, tried to calm us down. "Girls, shush-up. When the announcements are over, they'll start to call us. Find your places now and line up by club and age. You don't want to miss your name, do you?" Miss Lockhart also stood in the wings ready to give a stern look to any girls who got too excited.

What could be more thrilling and exciting for a young girl than to be a model in a fashion show? I was preparing for my first show and was as excited as if it were being put on by Coco Chanel herself. But it actually was the annual 4-H Fashion Show.

Mr. Bergen came backstage to give us some advice. "Just ignore those little butterflies, girls. They'll disappear the moment you start down the stage. Now don't forget to walk all the way over towards me at the podium before you do your turns. Break a leg."

Every year all the girl 4-H clubs in Suffolk County got together to show off the sewing projects their members had been working on. The fashion show judges had evaluated each girl's project; every part of the garment was scrutinized, down to measuring the seam allowances with a special ruler, to make sure it was perfectly constructed. My first project was the drawstring apron.

This was part of the first 4-H sewing project. We worked on these projects for months. To begin, each girl made a sewing box with brightly flowered calico. In this project we learned how to cook up flour, water and salt to make a paste and then how to measure to make a pattern from heavy brown paper. We carefully cut the calico from the patterns and pasted it on a shirt box. There was the sewing box that we would use for the rest of our 4-H career. Forty-odd years later I'm still using mine. We equipped the box by making things like needle holders, pincushions and scissors protectors out of felt. Mine were black and white felts sewn with fancy stitching in green and pink embroidery thread. With all our tools made, the next step was to start our sample book. Every time we learned a new technique we made a 3 x 5 size sample and pasted it in our notebook for future reference.

I still have my book, too. It has a green card stock cover titled *4-H Clothing Note Book.* It will soon be fifty years old and is getting sadly threadbare. I recently took it out to remind myself how to make bound buttonholes. Every time I look something up I am dismayed by the terrible spelling and typos.

At last we reached the part of the project where we really sewed something: the drawstring apron. Rather than going to Kresge's small fabric department for my first yardgoods purchase, my mom drove me up to Huntington Village to the special fabric shop stocked with any sort of cloth, notion, trim, and accessory that your imagination could desire. My instructions said to buy one yard of quarter-inch gingham. After great deliberation and debate we decided on a green and white check.

This type of apron is made from a long rectangle hemmed on all four sides. The ends of the top hem are left open and a drawstring, made into an inch and a half strip of the same gingham, is run through it and gathered around the waist. Not couture, but the height of fashion for a twelve-year-old. And believe me, it was harder than it looked. We had to learn to pre-shrink and straighten the grain. I soon discovered just how difficult it is to control a sewing machine. We were taught about exact measuring and absolutely straight stitching. From that skill we learned about the dreaded seam ripper. Every time a seam is sewn unevenly, easy to see on the gingham lines, our leader hands us the seam ripper, and the stitches are painstakingly taken out. By the time we finished, that apron was perfect.

೪ ೪

Finally it was time for all the months of hard work to pay off. My apron passed the evaluations with excellent comments. I had run into the Home-Ec room to give my apron a last minute touch-up with a hot iron, and it looked new and crisp. My mom had tied and retied the bow until it had two perfect puffs. Then we had made our way to the backstage area, and now the big moment was at hand.

We were all lined up, stifling giggles and stage fright, waiting offstage for our turn on the catwalk. Suddenly Mr. Bergen announced, "Now we have Mary O'Brien of the Huntington Station Blazers." I took a breath and strolled onto the stage, remembering to keep a buoyant, happy step as we had been instructed. When I got near Mr. Bergen, encouraged by his smile, I made my right turn downstage. "Mary's drawstring apron is cheery, Kelly-green-and-white gingham." At the stage edge, I did my half turn to the right, briefly pausing to show off the bow at the back, "Lovely, Mary. You did a great job." Then I half turned again, reminding myself to slow down, returned to center stage and continued off into the wings. With that it was over.

The fashion show continued. After numberless little girls modeled their aprons, the more advanced skirts and blouses were shown off, followed by the oldest girls in their tailored outfits and formal dresses. I would be returning year after year, finally in my own tailored herringbone suit with perfectly executed bound buttonholes. Edgar Bergen continued as Master of Ceremonies for many years and I learned what "break a leg" meant, but there was never another show where I felt as special and proud as I did with that little green check apron.

๛Mary O'Brien๛

Aspects of Renovation๛

"No, there is no way that you can leave the toilet four inches above the floor."

I am gripping the phone, trying to keep my voice steady, even though I want to start screaming at this plumber. Two days ago he called from the job and he told me I would have to raise the floor "a bit." I said, "Fine, I'll just have the carpenter put down a quarter of an inch of plywood." Perhaps he did not want to seem argumentative, or maybe he felt it would be better for him if I found out that a quarter of an inch was not enough long after he had left the job. Of course, I am not actually speaking to the plumber, but rather to his office manager, because no one else in the office will get on the phone with me. I think they are waiting for me to calm down.

It started when I decided to have a little work done on my rental house. Just a small bathroom renovation. Soon I realized I needed to add a closet and a new front entry and repair some fire damaged walls and ceilings. From this simple beginning the first aspect of renovation, the mushroom factor, took over.

As the crew gutted the bathroom, one of the workers took out the door and door jamb, which then necessitated removing the trim on the kitchen side. He chipped some baseboard, so took that out, too. Somehow he just kept going with all the kitchen trim. Okay. As long as the baseboard is up, let's do this floor, too. The ceiling has cracks, which will look awful with the new floor. Okay to that, too—new ceiling. The next time I visit the job I find they have taken every cabinet and appliance out of the kitchen and put them in the hall...right in front of the access panel to the electrical box, but the ceiling looks flat and shiny.

I would like to mention right now that I love having these guys work for me. They do wonderful work at a fair price. I would like to add that they drive me crazy because they follow the adage, "If it's worth doing, it's worth doing right." My mother used to say that, and it drives me stark, raving mad. Sometimes the work needs to match its intended use and the budget. Money is no object for my carpenters. This is why another aspect of renovation is that it will cost more than you could ever dream and if you have a nightmare about the bills, try to read them and then double the price. You'll be closer to the true total.

While waiting for the front door project, they did the closet. One of many questions came up. What trim do you want to use around the closet doors? They didn't ask about doors because they had some paneled doors from a previous job and all the guys got together and, after much discussion, it was decided that they should be hung as sliding doors. Luckily I agreed, but this points to a third aspect of renovation: the decisions factor. Someone will ask you about every little thing. That is, except for the things they forget to ask you about. Or the things they decide on their own because they are sick of listening to your dithering over every single thing.

I went to Lowe's, found some nice trim and bought enough for the closet, kitchen and bathroom. A few days later I noticed there was not much trim left on the pile. I guess the expensive, beaded trim *does* look nice on the inside of the closet. It's nice the way it matches the outside…oh, well.

The choice of the new front door turned into a major research project. I went to the lumber yard, but none of their catalogs had anything remotely similar to my Eastlake Victorian, two-inch-thick double doors. A special order quote came back with a reasonable price, but I noticed that they planned to use finger-jointed wood. I don't think so! Then I started asking around for advice. This led me to the next aspect of renovation: Everyone has an opinion. And they want to voice it, and, further, they are insulted when you don't take the suggestions that you're offered. Tenants all had a different vision as to how the house should look. It went from the paranoid tenant's wish for a reinforced steel door to the recommendation that I install a modern glass door with tinted sidelights. Friends called and said, "I was driving past your house and noticed you're doing some work. I have an idea..." One afternoon I saw two neighbors on their daily walk. They were stopped in front of the house and were having an argument about what color they should suggest that I paint the house. I ducked into the backyard before they saw me.

Luckily, I did get one bit of advice that paid off. An architect friend who is renovating her own Victorian told me about a great millwork company for a custom door. I said I was unsure of the style, and she quickly solved the problem. "This is a historic house. Recreate exactly what was there originally." Whew! That was easy!

The new doors came. They are smooth, warm Douglas fir, with gently rounded and beveled insulated glass. They were delivered by a tractor trailer truck longer than my front yard and packed in their own crate. They also are not finished. This brings up the fifth aspect of renovation that I want to discuss: Nothing is ever finished. Woodwork must be stained or painted. Appliances must be unwrapped from the protective films and tape and then always need cleaning. All of a sudden you realize that hundreds of new items must be applied: curtain rods, towel bars, switch plates. It was too dirty at the job-site to stain and varnish the doors, so for the last week I have had a mini shop set up in my family room. My own stain recipe and four coats of varnish have made them glow.

Now, let's get back to my plumber so we can get to the last aspect of renovation that I will consider: the disaster — the thing that no one foresaw, such as the recent national sheetrock shortage. Or it might be the problem that only could be found after the work started, such as rotten joists or the entire addition that the previous owner put on using only 2 x 3s on twenty-inch centers. Or it could be the plumbing work that was going so smoothly on Thursday; then on Friday the master plumber is called off the job to answer a frozen pipe emergency, and the helper is allowed to finish up the job 'cause *what could go wrong?* And then he puts the toilet flange four inches above the floor. That's where we are now, but the senior plumber is coming over later this week to "see what he can do about it."

Tomorrow the carpenters are planning on installing the new door. Pray for me.

❧Mary O'Brien❧

Face Off❧

"You will pay. You *will* pay," Kitty just keeps repeating, "You ate the food. You will pay."

She is standing to my right, yelling at the customer, her voice high-pitched, drenched in tension, frantically swinging her head as her hands fling gestures towards the man. The streetlight makes sparkles on her long, blond ponytail as it flies around her face.

"Ten dollars and forty-eight cents. Ten dollars and forty-eight cents."

"Leave it, Kitty. He doesn't have to pay. It's all right." I hiss to her, never taking my eyes off the customer's.

I'm standing in the middle of the sidewalk, staring up at the huge man opposite me. The streetlight shining from over his shoulder has put his face in shadow, but I can easily make out his eyes. He is staring at me. I am staring right back at him. We keep our eyes locked on each other, but in my peripheral vision I can still see the gun. A small revolver. He has it at waist level, under his coat, snug up against his body. Kitty can't see it, but I can. It's pointing at me.

"Kitty, he doesn't have to pay." I keep my voice low and even, trying to calm the situation.

"Yes he does. I'm not going to be stiffed for this."

McCann's on 33rd Street in Manhattan is one of those sports bar/restaurants that dot the city by the hundreds. McCann's, though, is special because it's a half block from Madison Square Garden and the Felt Forum. By day it's a busy, but staid, lunch joint for the garment district workers and shoppers—Macy's is just north one block. At night, though, if there's a big game or a hot concert, the place is packed with fans—some just got off the subway at the corner— or, for fans from the "burbs," off the trains at Penn Station across 8th Avenue. They have forty-five minutes to gobble a burger and down as many of our beers, at $5 less than the Garden's, as they can. The clientele might be wild, but Mr. McCann is there and keeps the security pretty tight. The manager, Reuben, never lets anyone mess with us.

Currently at the Garden the Rangers face the Islanders for the Stanley Cup playoffs. Fervent Long Island hockey fans have rolled off the trains to support their team against every Rangers fanatic in the city. Before the games we are many people over the legal occupancy and the place is out of control. Kitty, Carol and I have decided to serve only burgers and draft beer. We just squeeze through the crowds, trays held high, "Burgers, four dollars, drafts, buck apiece." We wear whistles on chains around our necks and blast them to get the guys' attention as we try to maneuver through the mob.

By the eight o'clock Face-off they have swarmed back out, cheering their way down to 7th Avenue. The place is empty except for a few professional bookie types, sitting in a side booth finishing up paperwork. A bit later I notice that only one remains, and when he gets up and goes out the door Kitty whoops, "No way," and in a flash is out after him. Curious, I follow her and catch up with them near the 6th Avenue corner.

"No one's stiffing me on the check," shrieks Kitty, "You've gotta pay."

He tries to push past her so I jump in front of him, blocking his path.

"Hey," he snarls, "I thought the other guys paid."

"Well, they didn't, and now you will. You *will* pay," repeats Kitty, her voice becoming higher pitched, tense.

Now that I'm in this situation I can't just turn around and walk back to the restaurant. I'm getting a little freaked because the guy looks like he knows what to do with that gun, and Kitty just keeps on. She's so shrill that I can see that he is getting a little tense too.

There are a few straggling groups of shoppers and tourists still on the street, but no one is paying any attention to our little exchange.

My mind becomes hyperactive. I notice that the night is mild. I think, "Thank God," since we only have our uniforms and Rangers shirts on. I take in the customer's brown suede bomber jacket, it's nice, and notice that the gun hand is still as a rock. Not Kitty though, when will she realize that she's the only one still talking? My mind wonders when will Rueben notice we're gone and come out after us. Stupid not telling him. I've got to get someone's attention. I put the whistle up to my lips, ready. The customer flicks his eyes over to Kitty, then back to me.

I can see a couple of guys approaching us. As they get twenty feet away I say in a loud voice, louder than I had intended, "Just 'cause you don't want to pay the bill is no reason to shoot us." Yeah, I think, lame, but I have nothing better. They hear and, without breaking their stride, change course to the other side of 33rd Street, but the customer can't see that. His lips give a little snick of a smile and he suddenly shoves past me. He throws a ten to Kitty and says to her, "Your friend has a big mouth," then disappears down Sixth.

I grab Kitty just as she begins to shout, "And what about the tip?"